Evergeti...

St George Monastery
Jerusalem

Published by: Virgin Mary of Australia and Oceania 2019 ©
info@athletis.com.au
www.oceanitissa.com.au
https://www.youtube.com/c/LookIntoMyWorld

All rights reserved. The material in this book may not be reproduced or distributed, in whole or in part, without the prior written permission of Virgin Mary of Australia and Oceania ©.

Translated from Volume 2 of the Greek edition.

Our books available on Kindle or Amazon Print. Please note that if you are in Australia and you are trying to purchase from Amazon USA that it will say the book is unavailable. You must use the Amazon website located in the country you live.

The **Philokalia Volume 5** by the Holy Monastery of St George, Jerusalem
Available for preorder.
Go to www.oceanitissa.com.au to subscribe for updates on when books are being released.

In the Footsteps of Jesus: Orthodox Holy Land by the Holy Monastery of St George, Jerusalem
Available for preorder.

Homilies by St Nektarios Volume 1 On Great Lent by the Holy Monastery of St George, Jerusalem

Homilies by St Nektarios Volume 2 On Concern for the Soul by the Holy Monastery of St George, Jerusalem

Homilies by St Nektarios Volume 3 Words of Eternal Life by the Holy Monastery of St George, Jerusalem

Homilies by St Nektarios Volume 4 The Priestly Engolpion by the Holy Monastery of St George, Jerusalem
Available for preorder.

Homilies by St Nektarios Volume 5 Christian Ethics of the Eastern Orthodox Church Part 1 by the Holy Monastery of St George, Jerusalem
Available for preorder.

Gerontikon Volume 1 by the Holy Monastery of St George, Jerusalem

Evergetinos Volume 1 by the Holy Monastery of St George, Jerusalem

The Monastic Rule of St Basil the Great by the Holy Monastery of St George, Jerusalem

The Way of a Pilgrim and the Pilgrim Continues His Way by the Holy Monastery of St George, Jerusalem

Fountain of Life Volume 1 by the Holy Monastery of St John, Perth

The Spiritual Life in the World by the Holy Monastery of St John, Perth

The Prodigal Son's Brother by the Holy Monastery of St John, Perth

Orthodox Prayer Book – The most extensive book of prayers available! by the Holy Monastery of St George, Jerusalem

Orthodox Daily Prayer Book by the Holy Monastery of St George, Jerusalem

Before and After Holy Communion Prayers: Orthodox Prayer

The **Life of Saint Anthony** the Great **by St Athanasius the Great**

The Service of the **Small Paraklesis to the Most Holy Theotokos**

Sayings of the Saints: Orthodox Spirituality **by the Holy Monastery of St George, Jerusalem**

Orthodox Colouring Book by the Holy Monastery of St George, Jerusalem

Please purchase and support our ministry in translations.

Principle 1
That those who humble themselves are honorable before God.

I. From St. Palladius

In Tabenna there is a women's monastery with about four hundred sisters, across from the men's monastery. At this monastery there was a virgin called Isidora who feigned foolishness for the sake of Christ, and humbled and abased herself. The sisters were so disgusted with her that they would not even share meals with her, but she accepted this with joy. Indeed, her virtue was exceedingly profitable to the monastery: she did all kinds of service, and like a slave was attendant to their every need, serving them with the utmost meekness. She was, as it were, the sponge cleaning the community. For as the Lord once said, "Whoever would be great must become the slave of all" (cf. Mt. 20:26-7). Also, "If anyone thinks he is wise, let him become a fool" (cf. 1 Cor. 3:18).

While the other nuns were tonsured and wore mantles, she had a rag tied round her head and served in this manner. None of the four hundred nuns had ever seen her eat, not even a single piece of bread, but the crumbs that she would collect from the tables and dishes were sufficient for her. Her feet were always unshod, and she never insulted anybody, neither did she boast or ever say anything small or great[1], even though she was insulted, beaten, cursed, and loathed by many of them.

On account of Isidora's sanctity, an angel appeared to St. Piteroun, a very experienced and virtuous hermit, and said to him, "Why do you think highly of your accomplishments and piety, living in this place? Do you wish to see a woman more pious than you? Go to the convent of the Tabennesiotes, and you will find there a woman with a crown upon her head. She is better than you: indeed, pushing through that crowd of people,

---

[1] Find better phrase: e.g. "Never said a mumblin' word" - "neither did she ever mumble or shout back, …"

she serves everyone uniquely, never letting her mind depart from God, even though they revile her. You who live in this place, on the other hand, are thinking about cities in your imagination, even if you never see civilization."

So Piteroun the Great arose and went to Tabenna, where he asked the elders for permission to visit the women's monastery. As he was held in honor among the Fathers and experienced in asceticism, they crossed the river and brought him there with confidence. Upon his arrival, the great saint sought to see each and every nun. All of the nuns gathered, yet the one he was looking for was not present, so he said, "Bring me *all* of the sisters."

"We are all present," they replied.

"There is one missing: the one whom the angel showed to me."

"There's one in the kitchen... A fool," said one nun.

"Bring her that I may see her too," insisted the saint. But the nun didn't obey, perceiving the reason why he wanted her (for perhaps it had also been revealed to her). Nevertheless, others dragged her in with force, saying, "Piteroun the Saint wants to see you" (indeed, he had the reputation of a saint among them).

Thus, as she was being led in, as soon as the great saint beheld her face and the rag on her head, he fell at her feet, saying, "Bless me, holy mother!" But she falling before him replied, "*You* bless me, reverend father!" The onlooking nuns were all astonished and said to him, "Abba, don't suffer this shame, since she is a fool."

"You are the ones who are fools. She is better than me and you. She is an *ammas* (that is, a spiritual mother), and I pray that I may be found worthy along with her on the Day of Judgment."

Upon hearing this, all the nuns fell down before him, weeping and confessing how they had grieved the holy woman in various ways. One said, "I was always mocking her," and another, "I ridiculed her humble attire." Other sisters followed, confessing,

"I often spilled the dish-water on her,"

"I gave her wounds,"

"I hit her with my fists,"
"I would often stuff mustard herbs in her face."

They all plainly admitted the various insults they had given her. After he had accepted their confession, St. Piteroun along with Isidora prayed on their behalf. He then beseeched the honorable servant of Christ to pray for him, and departed.

That holy woman, honored by God, was then greatly honored and cared for by all the nuns. But after a few days she could no longer bear the glory and honor that she received from the whole sisterhood, along with their apologies, and so she secretly left the monastery. As to where she departed to, where she hid herself, or where she died, no one ever found out.

II. From St. Gregory the Dialogist

St. Aecytius, who was found worthy of great gifts from God and led many souls to the Lord through his teaching and preaching, as the Lord commanded, used to dress in the humblest garments. Indeed, when he greeted strangers with a prostration, they looked at him with contempt and refused to return the greeting. Whenever he went on a journey to another place, it was his custom to take the most pitiful horse in the monastery. He used reins without bits, and instead of a saddle he sat on a sheepskin. He placed the Holy Books in a leather sack and wherever he went he would open up the spring of Scripture and thus nourish the spiritual soil.

The report of him came as far as Rome, but some that were motivated by envy spoke to the Patriarch against him and they didn't cease to accuse Aecytius him until they had persuaded him to send Julian, a church official, to bring the holy man to Rome. Julian went in haste to Aecytius' monastery where he found the chief monastics and spoke with them, inquiring as to where the abbot was. They told him, "He is in the valley farther down, collecting hay."

So the official sent his servant, who was extremely conceited and prideful, in order to summon the holy man. The servant found the brothers who were harvesting and demanded, "Where is Aecytius?" And as soon as he perceived which one of them was Aecytius, he was seized by an immeasurable fear: he began to shake and tremble and was hardly able to walk. He approached the saint, fell at his feet, and announced the arrival of his master to the monastery. The man of God put on his sandals, tied them, placed his sickle on his back and went on his way.

When Julian was informed by his servant that this man was Aecytius, he was disgusted with his appearance and, in his arrogance, he even hesitated to speak with him. But as he drew nearer to the saint, an immense fear took hold of him and in his trembling, he managed only to announce his reason for coming. Being humbled in this manner, he prostrated before the knees of the saint and asked for him to pray on his behalf. But Aecytius, after he had first raised him up, blessed him and insisted that they should go to the Patriarch together at once. "For indeed," he said, "if we do not go today, then it will be impossible for us to leave tomorrow." But Julian protested, "I am exhausted from the journey, father; I cannot go back today!" Thus being constrained by the official, they spent the night at the monastery.

On the following day, just as the day began to dawn, a servant from the Patriarch arrived and commanded Julian not to dare remove the servant of God from his monastery. When he was asked the reason why, he reported that the Patriarch had a divine vision that very night and was filled with fear for having summoned this servant of God. Immediately Julian went to Aecytius, saying, "Our father the Patriarch has requested that you not go through this trouble." But Aecytius was saddened, "Did I not tell you yesterday that if we weren't to depart at once, we wouldn't be able to go at all?"

Out of love, Aecytius kept Julian at the monastery and even provided a reward for his labor even though he sought none, and he then sent him off in peace.

Know, therefore, Peter, how much glory belongs to those who are reviled by others in this present life. For they are numbered among the citizens of the heavenly homeland, while those who through pridefulness justify themselves before men and are puffed up with vanity are found to be far from the sight of God. Therefore Christ reproves such as these, saying, "You are those who justify yourselves before men," (Lk. 16:15) and what follows.[2]

III. From the Life of St. Gregory the Wonderworker[3]

Once when many people were gathered in the neighboring city of Komana, some of them came to the wondrous Gregory and they honored him with an invitation to their church for an ordination to the priesthood, and the great saint came obediently to their summons. There they were [expressing] their opinions as to who seemed to be most distinguished in oratory and nobility and other marks of pride, and they cast their votes, nominating each another.

The great saint, however, waited for God to give a special counsel for this affair. Just as Samuel remembered not to be distracted by physical beauty and greatness when he was assigned with chrismating a king for Israel, but rather to seek a royal soul even if it happen to be in a humble body, in the same way Gregory looked beyond the interests and concerns of those who were voting, but looked to one thing only: Who, even before the proclamation, had the bearing of a priest through an attentive and virtuous life?

Thus as the others brought forward with applause the candidates they had voted for, he ordered them to inspect the way of life of the humbler people of the city, for it was possible to find among them one who had more spiritual wealth than these prideful men. But one of the men, considering the judgment of the saint ridiculous, said that it would be disdainful of their decision to vote if, while rejecting those distinguished through their education, rank, and the apparent report of their way of life, they were to consider bakers more worthy of the grace of the priesthood. He mocked the saint and said, "If you

---

[2] "You are those who justify yourselves before men, but God knows your hearts. For what is highly esteemed among men is an abomination in the sight of God." (Lk. 16:15, NKJV)

[3] (Written by St. Gregory of Nyssa in AD ... - confirm)

demand that we ignore those who have already been chosen by the city and raise to the office of the priesthood someone from the crowd, how about you call on Alexander the charcoal-maker to become a priest? If he seems good to you, we can all agree while the whole cities gathered here together."

Saying these words, he ironically voted for Alexander, accusing and despising the lack of judgment in what the saint had said. But from what had been said the idea occurred to the saint that perhaps it was a sign from God that this Alexander had been mentioned as a candidate. Thus he inquired, "Who is this Alexander you've mentioned?"

Then someone laughed and brought him forward from the group of candidates; he wore pitiable clothes that didn't even cover his whole body. Moreover his appearance clearly gave away his profession, as his hands, face, and skin were blackened with coal. And while the situation was an occasion of laughter for the rest, what with Alexander standing in their midst, it produced much astonishment to the insightful eye of the saint. For here was a man who, in such poverty and with such little concern for his body, saw only himself [as he was]. Indeed, this man even rejoiced in those things which appeared ridiculous to untrained eyes, and that's [where he stood]. [In fact,] he hadn't come upon this life of poverty out of necessity, but rather the man was a *philosopher*, as the remainder of his life demonstrated. For he finished the course of his life through martyrdom by fire. [He avoided the attention of people and his life surpassed those things that are considered important among men. He preferred nothing to that higher and true life which was his desire. Indeed, he had devised that life in secret in order to attain to his goal of a virtuous life. *difficult passage*]

Thus, while he was yet blooming in his youth, he hid himself behind this ignoble profession as if behind some ugly mask. For in his prudence he considered it dangerous to make apparent the beauty of one's body, understanding that this has been the occasion of serious falls for many people. Consequently, so as not to suffer anything undesirable or to bring about any cause of passion to ill-disposed eyes, he put on this ugly disguise and voluntarily practiced charcoal-making. Thus he exercised his body in virtue by means of labors, and he concealed his beauty with the filth of charcoal. Moreover, what he gained from these labors he put to the service of fulfilling the commandments.

St. Gregory met with Alexander away from the council and learned everything about him with accuracy. He then entrusted Alexander to those who were around him and told them what they were to do. He himself returned to the council and taught those who had been selected beforehand with discourses concerning the priesthood, as well as that manner of life which is characterized by virtue. While discoursing upon these subjects he occupied his listeners until the others had completed the task he had given them. They arrived with Alexander, who had been bathed and washed from the filth of smoke, and dressed in the robes of the saint (for this is precisely what he had told them to do).

When everybody turned toward him, they were amazed by what they saw. "You have suffered nothing out of the ordinary," the teacher began telling them, "in being deceived by your eyes and basing your judgment of the good on the senses only. Indeed the senses are an erroneous criterion for the truth of things. The senses by themselves prevent us from entering into the depth of truth. That demon which is the enemy of piety loves when the *chosen vessel* (cf. Act 9:15) remains unrecognized, concealed by ignorance, lest it come to the average person who might destroy [the devil's] tyranny.

Having said these things he brought the man before God for the priesthood, and conducted the ordination by grace in the canonical manner. All now looked to the new priest who was asked to give a homily before the church. Alexander showed at once, at the very beginning of his priesthood, Gregory's unmistaken judgment concerning him; for his speech was full of intelligence, although lacking in the embellishment of verbal eloquence.

Hence a certain proud young man who was distinguished for his Athenian eloquence ridiculed the plainness of Alexander's speech, since it wasn't ornamented with the superfluity of the Attic style. And they say that he was instructed in a divine vision, wherein he saw a flock of doves shining with an unusual beauty and heard someone telling him, "These doves belong to Alexander (whom you mocked.)"

IV. From the Life of St. Marcellus

The divine Marcellus, who was originally from Apameia[4], settled at the Monastery of the Akoimitoi (Sleepless), so-called on account of its unceasing successions of doxology unto God. Having been received there, after some time he was given the *schema* of the monks by the Abbot Alexander. Before coming to the monastery, there was a tonsured monk by the name of Jacob who had been known to Marcellus outside the monastery. Jacob waited on the Abbot Alexander, being the first among his disciples. Not much time passed before Marcellus exceeded in discipline and virtues not only the others, but also Jacob. Thus he was especially dear to Alexander.

When by the purity of his mind he foresaw the end of the Abbot's life, and similarly anticipating that the vote for the abbacy was going to fall on him, he feared lest a young man be given authority over his elders and there be lost that congenial order in which he rejoiced. For this reason, and on account of his *extreme moderation*, he left the monastery without anyone's knowledge. After a short time, when the holy Alexander had departed from this life, Marcellus' name was immediately on everyone's lips, and the brethren were greatly distraught when they discovered that he was no longer there. Accordingly, even though they voted for him, since he was nowhere to be found it was decided that the abbacy would go to John, a man with gray hair and understanding. Upon learning these things, Marcellus returned to the monastery and cooperated with the Abbot John, becoming to him his right hand, as it were, and contributing to the excellent administration of the monastery.

---

[4] Apameia

Once, while Marcellus was away on a journey, certain rumors about him came to John. On the one hand, the wiser monks wondered about Marcellus' behavior since he seemed to have carelessly avoided receiving the rule and throne of the monastery. On the other, the frivolous monks who were ignorant of the greatness of Marcellus' soul were saying that Marcellus fled the glory precisely out of vainglory. They also claimed that the reason why Marcellus was now gone from the monastery was because he saw that John was preferred over him, and he didn't want to appear second to him.

When John heard the report of this, he wished to persuade the monks not to form a bad opinion of someone so carelessly, and also to show them the great height of humble mindedness to which Marcellus had attained. Thus he said to them, "It is on the basis of works, my children, that judgment ought to be determined." And uttering nothing more than that, he thought of an idea: when Marcellus returned, he would give him the most contemptible kind of service, namely taking care of the donkey. And so as soon as Marcellus had returned to the monastery, the Abbot assigned to him this task that seemed utterly despicable in everyone's view. However, in response to this Marcellus demonstrated clearly his *extreme moderation*: for he did not only receive this assignment with rejoicing, but he considered even greater and nobler [than what he had done before].

In this way, they say, he gladly took up his new obedience, and inasmuch as he considered it [spiritually] profitable, he asked to receive a guarantee that he wouldn't be removed from this assignment. And he was not only saying this but really practiced it. Neither did he practice it for any short period of time, and they saw that his fervor to perform these tasks only continued to increase. He kept up this labor until they had all become suppliants to him, begging him to leave this manner of work and to forgive them. For it was absurd for this kind of man, who was worthy of guiding the *rational fold* and would bring great benefit to them, to remain instead with this contemptible job that anybody could do.

V. From the Gerontikon

1. It is said that for three years Abba Pambo continually asked God, "Do not give me glory on earth." And so God gave him glory such that others were unable to look into his face on account of its glory, for it shone brilliantly. Abba Sisoes and Abba Silouanos also had this gift.

2. Abba John the Dwarf said that there was once a certain spiritual elder who had hidden himself although he was known in the city and had much glory. This elder was once informed that one of the saints was about to die, and was invited to greet him before his repose. But he thought within himself, "If I go out by day, people will follow me, I will be given glory, and I will have no rest among them. Therefore I will depart under cover of darkness and escape everyone's notice. So he departed from his cell secretly, and lo! two angels with lamps were sent from God and appeared at his side. Thus the whole city saw this glory and followed after him in haste. And the more he wanted to escape this glory, the more glory he was given, according to what is written: "Everyone who exalts himself will be humbled, and he who humbles himself will be exalted" (cf. Mt 23:12).

3. Abba Isaac said, when I was younger, I stayed with Abba Kronios, and never did he tell me to do any work. Even as he was aging and had a tremor, he would rise and bring me the water jar, just as he did for everyone. I also lived with Abba Theodore of Phermi, and neither did he ever tell me to do anything, but he always prepared his own table and would say, "Brother, if you want, come and eat." But I told him, "Abba, I came to you to be benefited, and how is it that you do not tell be to do anything?" But he was always silent.

For that reason I left and told the elders, who came to him and said, "Abba, this brother came to your holiness to be benefited. Why is that you do not tell him to do anything?" And he replied to them, "Am I a superior that I should give him orders? I won't tell him to do anything. But if he likes, whatever he sees me doing, let him do likewise." So from then on, I learned to anticipate and to do whatever he was about to do; and whatever he did, he did in silence. Hence, this is what he taught me: to be in silence.

4. Abba Peter used to say that because Abba Macarius acted blamelessly towards all the brethren and humbled himself before all, there were some that complained, "Why do you treat yourself this way?" He answered, "For twelve years I have served my Christ that he might give me this gift and are you now requesting that I abandon it?"

5. Abba Poemen said, "If you humble yourself, you will find rest in whatever place you live."

6. It was said that Abba Peter and Abba Epimachos were companions at the Monastery of Raitho. Once when they were eating at the church, some [brothers] constrained them [by mistake] to go to the trapeza for the elders, and with much difficulty Abba Peter finally went by himself. When they had finished and got up, Abba Epimachos asked him, "How did you dare go to the trapeza for the elders?" Abba Peter said, "If I had sat with you all, the brothers would have made me bless first as a superior because I am older. But just now having gone to be with the Fathers, I was younger than everybody and consequently I had more humility in my thoughts."

7. Whenever Peter, a priest at Dion, prayed with others, he was compelled to stand in front of them on account of his priesthood. So out of humility he would stand behind them when he heard confessions, as is recorded in the life of Abba Anthony, and he did this without upsetting anybody. [**]

8. One elder said, "Either go into refuge by departing from people, or think little of this world as a child, making yourself a fool for the most part [temporal]."

VI. From Abba Cassian

1. There was a certain young man who was dignified in the world, and wealthy. He was the son of illustrious parents, was educated in the most important subjects, but ultimately he abandoned his own father (cf. Gen 2:24 LXX) and all his

secular eminence and rushed to the monastic life. In order to test his faith and humility, his Abba gave him the task of carrying ten baskets and selling them in his own city. What's more, he was to sell them not all at once, but one by one. And this he did with all patience and humility: he placed the baskets on his shoulders, sold them one at a time, and he didn't bring to mind either the shame, or the illustriousness of his birth, or the apparent dishonour of this act. For he was earnest to prove himself an imitator of Christ's humility.

2. And we beheld another one of the Fathers, Abba Pinouphrios, a man arrayed with all the virtues, and a priest and Abba of a large coenobium in Egypt, near the city of Panepho.

Seeing that he was glorified and honored by everybody for his culture, his old age, and his counsel, and how he was no longer able to exercise himself in feats of humility which he was formerly able to exercise through his much-loved obedience, he secretly left his own monastery and retreated by himself to the farthest parts of the Thebaid. After removing his *schema* and putting on worldly clothing, he went to the coenobium of the Tabennesiotes, intending to escape the notice of anyone there because of the multitude of its brethren and its location far away from his own monastery.

After some days had passed, he asked to be received into the monastery, and after much patience and persistence he was accepted by the Abba. The Abba gave to Pinouphrios (as to an old man who was capable of doing nothing else) the care and maintenance of the garden alongside another brother, to whom he was obedient. He thereby accomplished that humiliation and obedience which was so dear to him; and he was not content with that service only, but also performed earnestly those tasks that seemed strenuous to the others.

In this way he passed his life in hiding for three years, while his disciples searched for him throughout all of Egypt until he was recognized by one brother who happened to be there. Upon seeing the Abba and making out the features of his face, he still doubted and had to hear his voice to be sure. He couldn't be sure from his appearance, for he saw that this was a man who was quite aged, holding a trowel, cultivating the land, bearing the manure on his shoulders and spreading it on vegetable roots.

At any rate, as soon as he had diligently investigated the sound of the Abba's voice, he could understand that it was he, and he threw himself down at his feet to the great surprise of those who were present. For he did this to a man who was among them but a beginner; he had left the world just a short time ago and was considered the last [among them]. They were even more astonished when they learned [that his name was Pinouphrios], since he had a great reputation among them before. Hence, they asked for his pardon since in ignorance they placed him among the last. Begging him many times, he was sent back to his own monastery; he went back however involuntarily and grieving, since they didn't let him complete the humiliation and obedience that was dear to him.

After he had spent a short time at his monastery, he was enflamed once again by a longing for humility and submission. So he remained for a time and then left one night, not again to the Thebaid, but to a strange and foreign land. He went aboard a ship and departed for Palestine, hoping that he would finally escape successfully there. He stayed at the monastery next to the cave where Christ the Lord was born of the Virgin, and there he was received; and I happened to be spending time there as well. But neither was he able to hide for long there, according to the voice of the Lord, "a city set on a hill cannot be hid" (Mt 5:14, ESV).

For the brothers from Egypt went on a pilgrimage to the Holy Places and recognized him. With many supplications, entreaties, and tears, they persuaded him to return, and they all went back to his own monastery. I lived with this holy man for a short time in Egypt. I will tell the things that I once heard from him as he counselled a brother, whose acceptance into the monastery I attended. From these things you will get to know the man: how he was made worthy by God of such knowledge and from experience had an extraordinary understanding of every aspect of the ascetical life. So then, the author has written a work in praise of the Saint. Anyone who wishes to learn more will find [much] in that book, and in reading it he will be amazed.

VII. From Abba Isaac

Diminish yourself in all things toward all people, and you will be exalted above the rulers of this age. Despise yourself and you will see the glory of God in yourself. For wherever humility sprouts, there burgeons God's glory. If you struggle to be visibly of no account, God will make you to be glorified by all people; and if in your heart you have humility, in your heart God shows you his glory. Become contemptible in your righteousness; hasten to be disdained, and you will be filled with the honour of God. Hate honour, so that you might be honoured; honour flees from before the one who runs after her, but the one who flees from her she pursues and becomes a herald to all people of [his] humility. If you think little of yourself in order to be honoured, God will make you known. But when for God's sake you truly humble yourself he beckons all of his creatures to praise you; they will open before you the door of the glory of your Creator, and they will praise you because you are in truth made according to his image and likeness. Who has beheld a man who is splendid with virtues though he appears despised before men, who is both radiant in his life, wise in his knowledge, and humble in mind?

Principle 2
**That dishonor naturally gives rise to humility, while honor causes pride.
Therefore the humble minded rejoice when dishonored, but are grieved when they are given honor.**

I.   From St. Gregory the Dialogist

There once was an exceedingly devout man by the name of Constantine, who lived near the city of Ancona and served in the Church of Stephen the Protomartyr. Whenever he ran out of oil and had nothing with which to light the lamps, he would fill them up with water and place the usual wick in each of them. And having lit them, the water burned just as if it were oil.

Hear also of what sort of humility this man had; for the report of him had spread far [and wide] on account of the wonders that God worked through him, and many people from various places ran together to see him.

There was one farmer who came from afar in order to behold the sight (emphasis on appearance) of him. At that time the saint happened to be standing on a wooden stool to light the lamps. He was quite short from his old age, with an infirm body and an ugly appearance. The farmer sought diligently that someone point out to him the most devout man Constantine, and the people who were present [did so]. But he, as if defining virtue by the build of one's body, as soon as he saw that the man was so short and infirm he thought within himself that this couldn't [possibly] be that *reputedly great man he had heard about.

But when he had learned from many people that this indeed was the pious Constantine and not someone else, [still] from the shape and form of his body he was disgusted, and he said in ridicule, "I was expecting to see a *man*, but he has nothing of a man in him. Upon hearing this the man of God left the lamps and suddenly ran to greet the farmer and wrapping his arms around him he began kissing him sincerely and pronouncing blessings upon him for judging him in this manner. For he said, "You're the only one whose eyes are opened concerning me!"

Think then, Peter, how much humility this admirable man possessed, who [gave even more love] to the farmer that despised him. Therefore, the insult that is brought upon someone externally tests the internal disposition that is hidden within him. Just as the proud rejoice in honours, so the humble minded rejoice in dishonours and humiliations, and they are even glad when they suffer dishonours in the sight of many people. For when they are despised, they believe that the very judgment they had about themselves is confirmed; they are regarded as the kind of people that they take themselves to be.

II. From the Life of St. Ephraim

Among his other virtues, the marvellous Ephraim had this quality also: he greatly feared praises and not only did he avoid those who spoke highly of him but was even ostensibly displeased with them, just like someone would react to those who are mocking and insulting him: he would both blush and look to the ground, the color of his face would change, he would sweat a bit and remain entirely silent, just as if he were choked up by shame.

III. From the Life of St. Syncletica

Blessed Syncletica used to say to the women who came to her, ["Just] as wax melts before fire, so too the soul is destroyed by praises, losing its own strength. On the other hand, just as the cold makes the melted wax firm and solid, in the same way insults and humiliation strengthen the soul and [show it] to be secure. Hence the Lord says, "Rejoice and be glad when others revile you and persecute you," (cf. Mt. 5:11) and elsewhere it is said, "You have enlarged me in affliction" (Ps. 4:1 LXX).

Not only is this so, but indeed suffering derision naturally instills humble mindedness, the capital of virtues, into one's soul. Indeed these are the strands that out of which humble mindedness is made: curses, insults, wounds, derision; for someone to hear that he is witless, poor, miserable, sickly, procrastinating, irrational in speech, or ignoble in appearance:

These and the like [actually] strengthen humility, and our Lord suffered and heard such things. For they said that he was a Samaritan that had a demon (cf. Jn 8:48); he was struck, smitten with wounds, and called an evildoer and deceiver (cf. Mt. 27:63). So we too must imitate this humble mindedness in practice. For there are some who pretend to be humble by their outward appearance, and by this means they pursue glory. But they are known by their fruits (cf. Mt. 7:16-20). Hence, they cannot bear it when they are insulted just a little, but they immediately spit out their own venom like serpents.

IV. From the Life of St. John the Merciful

The wondrous Patriarch John had a nephew whose name was George. Once when he was insulted by one of the restaurant owners of the city, he was greatly irritated and bore it harshly. For what [caused the problem] was the great [difference of rank] between the two, that is George's relation to [such] a great man [as the Patriarch John] and the low rank of the offender who had shown contempt toward him. At any rate, the youth went to the blessed man by himself in tears and an aching heart, bemoaning the insult.

But the Saint, seeing his nephew overcome by passion, embraced him as he wished to [comfort] him, saying, "Did he actually dare to open his mouth against you? Did he really insult you who are so dear to me? The Lord be blessed, I will do something to him that will astonish (pass.) the city of Alexandria! When he had seen that at this statement his nephew [brightened up] (**), he said, "O child most dear to me, if you wish truly to be my nephew both in reality and in name, prepare yourself not only for insults, but if I [may] say so, even for scourges. For true nobility comes not from flesh and blood, but is characterized by the virtue of one's soul.

After this he quickly summoned the leader of the restaurant owners and ordered him to cease collecting the customary tax (or any other funds that were given to the church according to custom) from the very man who had insulted his nephew. [Learning of this] the people were astounded at the incomparable tolerance of [the Patriarch], and all came to the agreement that this was the "punishment" which was going to astonish all of Alexandria.

V. From the Narration of the Travels of St. John the Theologian

When the Apostle John was saved from that terrible shipwreck after forty days and washed ashore near Ephesus, he found me, Prochorus, standing on that shore just as he had told me to before the accident. Thus did he embrace me and give thanks to God, and afterwards we entered Ephesus and rested nearby the place named after Artemis, inside a bathhouse belonging to Dioscorides, a leading citizen of the city. John said to be, "My child, Prochorus, let no one in this city know who we are and for what reason we came here, until the Lord reveal us and we acquire boldness."

After saying these things, there came a serious lady named Romana who was under the employment of Dioscorides. She was in charge of the administration of his bathhouse. Everyone avoided her on account of her extremely harsh temperament. As she was overseeing the bath house, she caught sight of us and noticed from our miserable appearance that we were in need of bread and that because of our difficult situation we could be useful to her since we wouldn't ask for much compensation. So she quickly asked John, "Where are you from, man? And what is your religion?" He answered, "We are Jews by origin and Christians by grace, and we just survived a shipwreck." She then said to him, "Do you want to burn fuel for the furnace of the bathhouse, while your companion can work inside the bath?" And John accepted.

She brought us into the bathhouse right away and assigned these sorts of tasks to us, and for our daily nourishment she provided us with three measures of bread and four obols. However, on the fourth day of our stay there John showed a certain lack of skill in handling the furnace and he failed to reach the quota of fuel to be burned.

When Romana came and discovered this, she shamelessly struck John to the ground with her own hand, knocking him to the floor and cursing, "Peasant! Fugitive! Your bad luck, you exile! If you're so useless, why did you take on this work? You're just as deceitful as you look. I will be inspecting your work. You are a slave to Romana, and let it be proclaimed from here to Rome! From now on you are my slave. You won't be able to escape your master's hands; I can easily arrest you and destroy you if you ever dare do such a thing. Get rid of any devious thoughts then and as you have your mind set on food, attend to your work unless you want to be killed without mercy."

But John responded, "Ma'am, I only recently began this job and had no knowledge of it before; but time, which gives experience, will grant me skillfulness. The lady then departed, and there came to me the heavy darkness of despondency, since John was already enduring things in this harsh manner when we had only been staying in that place for four days.

Perceiving my despondency in the spirit, John said to me, "My child Prochorus, you know what manner of shipwreck befell us because of my hesitance when Asia fell to me as my lot. Moreover, it wasn't only we that suffered, but all the innocent people on that boat partook of my chastisement--they too were shipwrecked, but also saved by the Providence of God. Thus was I forty days at sea, being chastised so as to be obedient to God rather than to human understanding, until God in his usual compassion brought me to dry land.

"Since you understand these things, you must not despair, but rather give thanks in the midst of temptations. In fact, do not even regard the cold threats of this one lady as a temptation. Go then to the work that was appointed to you and perform it with the utmost care. For our Lord Jesus Christ, the Maker of all things, became for our sakes an example and model and revealed to us the reward for patience when he said, "By your patience gain your souls" (Lk 21:19).

By these words he rid me of the passion of despondency and restored me. On the next day Romana came and said to John, "Yet again I've heard many reports against you. They say that you're inattentive to your work and that you do this out of malice, so that I should fire you. But everything you're scheming is in vain, and you're only devising trouble against your own pate. If things really are as I suspect, I won't leave any of your limbs unmaimed; I'll thoroughly destroy them and leave you incapacitated.

In response to this John did not talk back. But Romana, interpreting John's meekness and silence as fright and stupidity, dealt yet more harshly with him, threatening and shouting, "Are you not my slave, you villain? What do you say? Do you not admit your bad luck? Speak! Answer me."

"Yes," said John, "We are slaves, both I and Prochorus who is with me."

When she caught these words, she immediately began taking motions against our liberty. She met with a certain lawyer and began preparing a case against us, saying, "I have caught two slaves who belonged to my parents. They ran away and I lost their contracts over the years. Now they have returned and they confess that they belong to me; may I make new contracts?" The lawyer told her, "If they confess that they are slaves to your ancestors in front of witnesses, you may."

John learned these things in the Spirit and said to me, "My child, Prochorus, you should know that this lady is attempting to obtain a written confession that will register us as her slaves and will be confirmed before witnesses. But have no sorrow in your heart because of this; rather, rejoice, for through it God will be glorified and will speedily reveal who we are.

After he said this, Romana entered and, taking John by the arm, she began to strike him and to say, "Bad slave! When your master enters, why do you not greet her and prostrate before her? It makes you look free. But you are a slave to

Romana. Right then she cursed and threatened, "You *are* my slaves, are you not?"

John said, "[Not once but twice have I told you, we are slaves." "*Whose* slave, you villain?" "We are doing the work of Another."

"Indeed, since it is *our* work you are doing, and you belong to *us*."

But John then said, "Both in writing and off the record we are confessing that we are slaves."

"Well, I want it in writing," she insisted, "and before witnesses."

"Worry not. If you so desire, do what seems right to you."

She proceeded to bring us to a public place near the sanctuary of Artemis, and there recorded our consent in writing before witnesses. Afterwards she brought each of us back to the work of the bathhouse that had been assigned to us.

Meanwhile, there had always been a certain demon that inhabited the bath, and three times a year he drowned unsuspecting visitors who came to bathe there. That night, the son of Dioscorides, Domnus, came in late from exercising to bathe. Suddenly, the demon rushed upon him and drowned him. When his servants entered and found him dead, they left weeping and saying, "Woe unto us, for our lord has drowned! What will we do?"

As soon as Romana heard what had occurred, she tore her hair covering and pulled at her hair, weeping and crying in utter distress, "Woe is me! What will I say, how will I answer to my lord Dioscorides when he learns of this? There is no consolation for such a misfortune. Perhaps he won't be able to bear the weight of it and will die, since my lord Domnus was his only begotten son. O great Artemis, help!"

She shouted these things and more of the same, even cutting her arms and striking her own face. In the meantime, John came back from his usual work and asked me, "What is this thing everyone is talking about? What has befallen the lady?" When Romana saw us speaking to each other, she ran and grabbed John and shouted, "You magician! The spells you did have been discovered! From the day you came here our goddess has abandoned us. Either raise the son of my lord, then, or I'll sunder your soul from your body this very hour."

John said to her, "What is this that is grieving you? Tell me."

And she, completely abandoned to her grief, raised her hand and hit him, saying, "Wicked slave, exiled for your wickedness! The entire city of the Ephesians knows what happened and you ask as if you did not know? The son of my lord Dioscorides died in the bath."

When he heard this, John appeared to me almost joyful, and having retreated for a little in prayer, he then went into the bath. He drove the unclean demon out of its home and brought the soul of the child back to its rightful home, the body. Taking Domnus by the hand, they both walked outside towards Romana and John said, "Receive the son of your lord alive and well, and be not distressed." As she saw what had occurred, Romana was shocked. She fell down at the feet of John, pleading for him to forgive her for all the terrible things she had committed against him. But he said, "Lady, believe in our Lord Jesus Christ, whose disciple and Apostle I am, and all these things shall be forgiven you."

"From now on, man of God, I will believe all the things that proceed from your mouth."

Meanwhile, one of the servants of Dioscorides announced to him the death of his son. From the unexpected calamity he suddenly fell down and died, as if smitten by a sword. When John learned of this, he came and raised him up too, and he baptised all who believed. Through these events, many Ephesians were added to the faith.

VI. From the Gerontikon

1. Once some brothers went to Abba Agathon, since they heard that he had great discernment. And wanting to test whether he would get angry, they said to him, "Are you Agathon? We hear that you're a fornicator and a prideful man." And he replied, "Yes, it is so." They continued, saying, "Are you Agathon, the babbler and slanderer?" And he said, "I am." And

again, they asked, "Are you Agathon, the heretic?" And he replied, "I am not a heretic."

So they inquired of him, "Tell us, why is it that, when we said so many things against you, you accepted them, but you did not bear this word?" He answered, "The first things I impute to myself, since they are profitable for my soul. But to be a heretic, that means separation from God. And having heard his word of discernment, they marvelled and left in an edified state.

2. One elder said, "Whoever praises a monk hands him over to Satan."

3. The elders used to say that once some dried figs were donated to the Skete, and since they weren't good quality, they didn't send any to Abba Arsenius so as to avoid insulting him. However, when the elder heard of this he did not come to the gathering but sent a message, "You have cut me off from receiving this blessing which God has given to the brotherhood, of which I am unworthy." And after everybody heard this, they were profited by the humility of the elder, and the priest delivered some figs to him and brought him to the gathering with joy.

4. They said concerning Abba Ammon that there once came some people who made suits against him, but the elder acted like an idiot, as it were. Indeed, one woman stood next to him and said, "This elder is a fool!" Hearing this, the elder said, "How many labours have I spent in the desert in order to obtain this foolishness? Will I let it be destroyed today because of you? Never."

5. There was once a meeting in Kellia concerning some matter, and Abba Evagrius spoke. Then a priest said to him, "We know, Abba, that you could have been a bishop and leader of many people in your country. But now you have your seat here as a foreigner." He, feeling compunction, was not disturbed, but nodding his head, he replied, "I spoke once, and I will not speak again."

6. Abba John once said, "Humility is the gate to heaven. Our Fathers, in enduring offences, entered the city of God rejoicing."

7. The same elder said to his brother, "Even if we are most wretched in the sight of men, let us however rejoice in this, so as to find honour before God."
He was always fervent in his spirit. Once, a brother came to his side while he was weaving and began praising his work, at which he grew silent. A second time he said a word of praise to Abba John, and again he was silent. But when the brother praised him yet a third time, Abba John replied, "From the moment you came in here you have removed God from me."

8. This elder was once sitting at Sketis with the brothers gathered around him, confessing their thoughts. One of the elders then said to him, "John, you are much like a prostitute who beautifies herself and in this way draws more lovers to herself." Abba John embraced him and said, "You speak the truth, father." Afterwards, one of his disciples asked him, "Are you not disturbed within yourself, Abba?" And he answered, "Not at all; as I am on the outside, so am I on the inside."

9. Abba James said, "Let the one who is praised reflect upon his sins, and let him consider that he is unworthy of what is said of him, and he will not be harmed so much by the praises."

10. They used to say about Abba Macarius that when anyone of the brothers would come to him treating him like a great and holy elder with reverence, he wouldn't say anything to him. If, however, one of the brothers came to him demeaning him with words such as, "Abba, when you were a camel-herder and gathered and sold nitrogen, didn't the supervisors used to beat you?" If anyone said this, he would speak to him with pleasure and answer any question that was asked of him.

11. They used to say about Abba Moses that when he became a priest and arrayed him with a white vestment, the

Archbishop told him, "Behold, you have become pure white, Abba Moses." But he replied, "So then, does the Pope ordain the exterior rather than the interior?" And the Archbishop, wishing to test him, told the other priests, "When Abba Moses enters the sanctuary, drive him out, but then follow after him to hear what he says." So when the elder entered, they chastised hm and drove him out, saying, "Get out of here, you Ethiopian!" And leaving, he said to himself, "They've done well to you, O black one... Since you have committed inhuman things, what are you doing among human beings?"

12. An elder said, "He who is honored beyond his dignity is much harmed. But he who is not honored by men in any way is glorified from above."

13. A brother once asked an elder, "Tell me something, that I may keep it and live by it." The elder told him, "If you are able to be insulted and bear it, that shall be greater to you than all the virtues."

14. One elder said, "He who degrades himself is not humble-minded, but rather the one who receives insults and dishonors from his neighbor with joy."

15. He also said, "If a man praises you to your face, bring to mind your sins and beseech him, saying, "For the Lord's sake, brother, cease praising me, for I am a wretch and cannot bear it." If the one praising you happens to be a great man, pray to God in your heart, saying, "Lord, shelter me from the praise and reproach of men."

16. Once Abba John the Dwarf was sitting in front of the church and the brothers sat around him sharing and examining their thoughts with him. Seeing what was going on, one of the elders was struggling with envy, and said to him, "Your pot is full of poison, John." And John replied, "Indeed it is so, Abba; and you have said this seeing merely my exterior. If you were to see the interior, what would say?"

17. A meeting once took place at Scetis, and the fathers, wanting to test Abba Moses, degraded him, saying "Why has this Ethiopian come into our midst?" Hearing this, he was silent. After they had dismissed the meeting, they asked him, "Abba, were you not disturbed just now?" And he said, "I was disturbed, but I did not speak."

VII. From Abba Isaiah

1. Abba Isaiah said, "If your brother answers you with a word that proceeds from weakness of soul, bear it with joy. And if you examine your thoughts with the judgment of God, you will find that you have sinned."

2. The abandonment of the soul to God gives birth to the capacity to suffer insolence without agitation. Her tears are protection from all things done by humankind. Refusing to blame oneself brings about an inability to withstand wrath.

3. The one who possesses humility is not concerned with the cursing of men. For the remembrance of his own sins becomes to him armor and protects him from wrathfulness and retribution, and he endures whatever may happen to him. For what kind of accusation of men could compare with the blame he has before God, or with his own sins which are before the face of God?

4. The one who is able to bear a harsh word from a difficult and unwise person, for God's sake and for the sake of making his thoughts peaceful: such is able to acquire peace of body, soul, and spirit. And when these three are in agreement, and cease their opposition to the law of the intellect, and when the captivity of the flesh is abolished, such a man will be called a son of peace, and the Holy Spirit shall make his dwelling in him. For he has come to belong to the Spirit, and shall not be separated from him.

5. Believe, brother, that insults and dishonors are a great gain and salvation for the soul, that is when they happen to you for the Lord's sake (cf. Mt. 5:11). Bear them readily and without distress, meditating thus, "I am worthy of suffering more than this on account of my sins, and I am being made worthy to suffer for the Lord, that through many afflictions and dishonours I may become an imitator of the Passion of my God, if even for a moment." And as often as you remember them that have afflicted you, pray on their behalf as for people who have brought great benefit to you, genuinely and from your soul, without murmuring anything against them.

6. And again, hate and deplore lust for power and glory, as well as the desire to receive praises from men, as dark death, destruction of your soul, and eternal torment.

7. Be strictly attentive to yourself, so that when someone afflicts you in anything and sorrow or anger are borne within you, you might be silent and keep yourself from saying anything but what is proper, until your heart is first mollified by prayer. Only in such a state, then, may you admonish your brother.

VIII. From Abba Mark

1. The cursing of men produces affliction in the heart, but it becomes an occasion for purity for the one who endures it. If you desire to receive praise from men without condemnation, you must first love reapproval of your own sins. In as much as someone experiences shame for the truth of Christ, he will be glorified a hundredfold by the multitude. It is better, nevertheless, to accomplish every good thing for the sake of things to come. [5] When you perceive a thought suggesting human glory to you, know with certainty that it is devising your shame.

---

[5] Perhaps here Abba Mark is saying that it is better seek future goods than to seek future glory.

2. Human praise is the root of shameful desire, just as the reapproval of malice is the root of temperance. It is not a matter of hearing these things only, but of accepting them. When you are hurt, or accused, or persecuted by someone, do not set your mind on the present, but look forward to the future, and you will find that what has happened to you has been the occasion of abundant goodness, not only in the present but in the age to come.

3. If you ever perceive that someone is praising you hypocritically, expect to hear a complaint from that same person within a short period of time. When you suffer dishonour among men, immediately bring to mind the gift of glory that comes from God. So then, on the one hand, if you are in the midst of dishonour you will remain undisturbed and without sorrow, and on the other hand, if you are in the midst of glory, you will [still] be found faithful and uncondemned when the Lord comes.

**4. When, by the good pleasure of God, you are being praised by the multitude, do not mix up any pretentiousness of yours in the economy of the Lord, lest you be rejected and fall into a contrary state.

When you see someone incapable of bearing the pain of many dishonours, you should know that he is suffering from the passion of vainglory, and is reaping the unpleasant crops of the seeds planted in his heart.

The lover of pleasure is grieved when he is accused and suffers evils, whereas the lover of God is grieved by praises and ambitious desires.

IX. From Abba Isaac

Endure degradation and humiliation with a good will, that you may acquire boldness before God. When a man endures every harsh word with [spiritual] knowledge (apart from those cases in which he has first sinned against the person who is speaking harshly with him), he takes onto his own head a crown of thorns; and blessed is he, for at a time he does not know, he will be crowned with incorruption. The perfection of humility is bearing degradation and every false accusation with joy. For the genuinely humble-minded person is not agitated when treated unjustly, nor does he make a defense concerning the thing in which was ill-treated, but he accepts the slander as if it were the truth. Nor is he anxious to convince people that he has been slandered, but rather seeks forgiveness.

Indeed there are some who have voluntarily drawn to themselves the name of intemperance, although they were not intemperate. Others went so far as to endure the accusation of fornication. Thus did they take on themselves, with tears, the burden of a sin they did not commit, and they sought out forgiveness, with weeping, from those very ones who unjustly accused and slandered them; and all the while, as they were entirely clean and pure, their souls were crowned. Others, to avoid being glorified for their virtuous state, kept it hidden and made themselves look mad while they were [really] seasoned with the divine salt and stable in their inner tranquility, so that on account of their utmost perfection, the Holy Angels proclaimed their noble and courageous deeds. You should not think that you are in possession of humility, then, when you cannot bear simply being accused. If, therefore, you wish to know whether you are humble-minded, try the things that have been said.

X. From the Gerontikon

Once, a brother who was a novice left Scetis and came to the Coenobium of the Tabennesiotes, where there were men who were nearly all saints and strict ascetics. And so after thirty days the brother went before the Archimandrite, saying, "Say a blessing for me, Abba, and let me go; for I am unable to stay here." The Father said to him, "Why, my child?" And he replied, "Because there's nothing to be accomplished here, neither is there any reward, since all the fathers are athletes, while I am a sinful man. So I am going to find a place where I will face derision and degradation: for there are the things that save a sinful person." Having heard this, the elder marvelled and perceived that he was a laborer [in the faith]. And so he let him go after saying the blessing, "Go forth, my child. Be brave, and let your heart be strengthened, and wait on the Lord" (Ps. 26.14 LXX, cf. 30.25).

XI. From Abba Zosima

1. Abba Zosima said, "There are many different motives for free will, and while one fervent will can offer itself to God within an hour, so too another will that is sluggish could wait fifty years before offering itself. Thus, when demons see that someone is insulted, dishonoured, injured, or that he has suffered anything and is in affliction (and not only when he has suffered evil, but that he is nobly resisting [a negative] emotion, they are greatly afraid. For they realize that he has made contact with the way of truth, and that he desires to walk according to God's commandments.

2. The same elder used to say, "If someone remembers the person that has afflicted, ridiculed, injured, or done any other terrible thing to him, he ought to remember the offender as a physician and to pray for him with his soul. But if he instead weaves thoughts against him, he conspires against his own soul as the demons do. Or rather he becomes a demon and opponent to himself, since he doesn't wish to be delivered from evil, but remains ill without a cure. For if he were not ill, he would not be suffering [so much] from the one afflicting or ridiculing him, who is in fact a physician sent to him by Christ, to reveal to him his passion though the insult or injustice.

"If he truly desires to be healed, he ought to regard his offender as a sort of benefactor and to receive from him the healing medicine which comes from Christ, and to give thanks for these things, even if they bring pain at that moment. For neither does a patient have any pleasure in surgery or cautery or cleansing, but he regards all such things with revulsion. Nevertheless, he persuades himself that it is impossible to be delivered from the illness without them and thus does he commit himself to the care of the physician, understanding that through a little pain he will be delivered from maladies and chronic illness.

"In like manner, the person who brings to you injury and insult is like a cauter of Jesus that delivers you from greed and pridefulness. If you do not tolerate these sorts of treatments, not only refusing to give thanks but even weaving thoughts a brother, then you are in effect saying to Jesus, 'I do not want to be healed by you. I don't accept your medicine. I would rather fester in my wounds.' And what, then, will the good Lord do? Know then, brother, that the one who flees from a temptation which is profitable, flees from eternal life.

3. "Indeed, Evagrius also used to say, 'I cast no blame on them that speak evil of me, but I even call them benefactors. Moreover, I do not drive away the physician of souls and the medicine of dishonour that is offered to my vainglorious soul. For I fear lest the Lord say of my soul, 'We tried to heal Babylon, but she was not healed' (Jer 28.9 LXX [51.9]). For our Lord, being good, gave us holy commandments for our evils, removing them, as it were, by cauters and cleansers. It is therefore impossible to be delivered from illness in any other way but by receiving the proper and attendant treatments.'"

4. He also used to say, "No one is lying but those who praise and bless me, and no one is telling the truth but those who blame and demean me. Neither do they say the whole truth, nor do they understand exactly all that is in my heart. If others were granted to see not all, but just a portion of the evils in me, they would turn away from me as from a filthy quagmire, a stench, or an unclean spirit. And even if all men were to become tongues for accusing me of my faults, I am convinced that even then my own dishonour could not be proclaimed. For if the righteous Job said, "I am full of dishonour" (Job 10:15 LXX), and nothing can be added to "full", what should I then say, since I am a sea of every evil?

With every sin the devil has humiliated us, and should we not recognize our own humble state? Those who know themselves destroy Satan who had destroyed them. Thus, as the Holy Fathers have said, when humility is brought down to Hades, it is raised up to Heaven, just as pride, when it exalts itself to the heavens, is brought down to Hades." He [who?] also used to say, "Who has ever persuaded a humble man to weave thoughts against another?"

Therefore every grievous thing a humble person suffers or hears is made into an opportunity to deride and dishonour himself, like the time when Abba Moses was cast out of the sanctuary and insulted by the priests, and he derided himself even more than they. If it ever occurs that a humble person is agitated on account of the insult or injustice that he has suffered, he turns directly to prayer, my means of which his heart is quickly soothed. Not only this, but in his agitation, he always afflicts and reproves himself, saying to his own soul, "Why are you mad, wretched soul? Why are you disturbed like crashing waves of the sea? By the fact that you are so disturbed, it is clear that you are ill. If you were not ill, you would not be suffering like this. Why, miserable soul, have you abandoned self-blame and instead blamed your brother, who has showed the illness that was hidden within you, unbeknownst to you until now?

Imitate Christ who did not speak back when others spoke against him and, while suffering, did not resist. Listen to him saying, and showing in practice, "I gave my back to scourges and my cheeks to blows; and I turned not away my face from the shame of spitting (Isa 50:6 LXX [AB]). And you, wretched one, because of one insult, you remain weaving countless thoughts against your brother, who has done good to you through this slight dishonour. And rather than perceiving this, you scheme against yourself as the demons do. What has the demon left to do, seeing all that you have done to yourself, foolish and wretched soul?" The elder also brought up the fact that every day we see the cross of Christ and we read of the passions he suffered for us, and we cannot bear even one insult? Truly, we have strayed from the right path.

5. Again, he used to say, "If someone were to live all the years of Methuselah[6], and not walk the right path that all the

Saint walked, which is the way of being dishonoured, injured, and bearing it all nobly, he will have made no progress in any goodness, small or great; all those years will have been wasted.

6. Again, he said, "Once a brother asked me, 'Abba, there are many commandments of Christ, but my nous is darkened, and I am unable to keep them all. Tell me then, what shall I do?' So I told him, 'Brother, do not be disturbed because of this. Rather, meditate thus, as much are you are able: Bear all that happens to you with thanksgiving, and in this way, you will accomplish all the virtues easily. For what kind of effort [does it take] to pray on behalf of on that grieves you? Is it like mining the earth? Or making a journey? Or crossing the sea? Or losing property?

'Give thanks when you are dishonoured, then, and you will have become a student of the Holy Apostles who during their travels rejoiced that they were made worthy to be dishonoured for Christ's name. And indeed, as pure ones they rejoiced on behalf of Christ's name, whereas we have need of dishonor because of our sins. And even if no one dishonours us, we are [in fact] dishonourable and cursed. For it is written, "Cursed are they that turn aside from your commandments" (Ps 118:21 LXX, AB). For it does not belong to all [to suffer only] for Christ's name, but only to the saints and to the pure, as I have said. But it belongs to us to bear gratefully the dishonours and insults we receive, and to confess that we are dishonoured for our evil deeds.

'However, this wretched soul, even though it knows its unclean deeds, and that it is worthy of suffering whatever it does suffer, fails to consider its own conscience and weaves [negative] thoughts against the brother, saying, *He said that to me, and dishonored me, and mocked me.* Thus the foolish and unwise soul does not follow sense, but plots against itself and performs the work of demons.

---

[6] Gen 5:27 LXX [AB] "And all the days of Methuselah, which he lived, were nine hundred and sixty-nine years, and he died."

'In the same way that a supervisor of crafts entrusts the work to his student and lets him work by himself, no longer needing to check on him all the time, but only coming to him at intervals to make sure he has not neglected the work or disappeared, so do the demons likewise: If they see a soul that is subject to them and accepts wicked thoughts easily, they entrust to it a satanic art, which is their own malice and wickedness, and they've no need to monitor the soul, knowing that this is sufficient for the plot and the destruction. Only on occasion do they come to check on the soul lest it has neglected the work which it received from them.'"

7. Again he used to say, "What is easier than to love all and to be loved by all? What comfort do the commandments of Christ not provide us with? But our free will does not act; if it were to act, by God's grace everything would be easy for it, and a small motion of our will draws God unto help, as I have often said. And virtue requires only our will, as the divine Anthony said.[7] There is no need for any toil when grace cooperates in everything. Thus, what kind of comfort does the meek and humble person not possess? Truly, "The meek shall inherit the earth, and shall delight themselves in the abundance of peace" (Ps 36:11, cf. Mt 5:5).

8. The same elder [Zosima] said, "At one point, there was one brother who lived with me and received his *schema* from me, and with my guidance he made much progress in the good [life]. But he was also spoiled, and he needed much care and sympathy because of this weakness of his. Once he came to me and said, 'My Abba, truly I love you!' And I told him, 'I have not yet found someone who loves me as much as I love him. You see, at present you are saying you love me, and I believe you. But if something happens that is not pleasing to you, you will not remain the same. But whatever I suffer from you, I will the remain the same, and nothing can separate me from my love for you.'

---

[7] St. Athanasius the Great, *Life of Anthony*, 20.

"A short time passed, and I didn't know what happened to him, since he no longer had his dwelling with me. He had begun saying many awful things against me, even shameful. When I found out all that he was saying about me, I said in myself,

'He is a cauter of Christ, and has been set to heal my vainglorious soul; he is really my benefactor.' Thus I remembered hm in my prayers as a physician and benefactor, and I prayed earnestly on his behalf, and [my reply to the brothers who] reported all that he said about me was, 'This brother knows my apparent evils, and not even all of them, but merely a few. He only says what he knows, since those evils that are hidden and that escaped his notice are innumerable.'

"After some time, then, he met me in Caesarea and would approach me according to the custom, with an embrace and a kiss, which I likewise returned, just as if nothing new had happened. And this did not happen once or twice, but often. That is, while he was saying these things against me, he would greet me with embraces. But I betrayed none of my suspicion to him, nor did I show any hint of grief, just as if, as I said, nothing of what he was saying had come to my attention.

"At one point, he came and greeted me in his usual manner when suddenly he fell down at my feet and held them, saying, 'Forgive me, Abba, for the Lord's sake, for I have said many terrible things against you.' But I raised him up and kissed him, and told him graciously, 'Will your grace remember that you once said you truly loved me, and I replied that I had never met anyone that loved me as much as I loved him? You know the rest of what I told you. Be sure then that none of what you were saying about me escaped my notice, but I also learned about where it was told and which people heard it. But I never said, *It is not so, as this brother says*, nor did anyone persuade me to say anything bad about you, but I would say to those messengers, *Everything he says is true and he says it out of love*, [taking it on myself], and I never ceased to remember you in my prayers.

"And a further proof of my love towards you is that once I felt a terrible pain in my eye, and then I remembered you, made the sign of the cross, and said, *Lord Jesus Christ, through the prayers of this brother, heal me!* And immediately I was healed.

"From then on, that brother had perfect trust in me and ceased all of his speaking against me, and he held me in much esteem and loved me."

Elder Zosima also added, "We cannot know when we are loved or honored by others, but rather we have lost this capacity of ours to discern. But if one bears with his brother while he, under the influence of the Enemy, is animated and directed by him, then when that brother comes to himself after a while and realizes his brother's tolerance, and how he bore with him patiently, he thanks him abundantly and comes to love him so much that he would earnestly lay down his life for him" (cf. Jn 15:13).

Principle 3
That it is necessary to avoid being lazy, and to do bodily labor, and that laziness is the cause of many evils.

I. From Palladius

A. When St. Pambo was nearing death, it's mentioned that he told the Holy Fathers, "From the moment I entered this desert, built my cell, and took my abode therein, not one day has passed when I did not engage in labor with my own hands, nor do I ever remember taking bread from anyone for free."**

B. I once happened to stay in Galatia at the same time as the God-beloved bishop Philoromus, a most ascetical and resolute man, whom Basil cared much for, since he was pleased with his austerity, harshness [of life], and the attentiveness he gave to his work. To this day Philoromus has not ceased to put down pen and paper, although he is eighty years old.

This blessed man once said, "From the time of my baptism to this hour, I haven't taken bread from anyone, but from the labor of my own hands I have given two hundred coins to the lepers.

He went on a pilgrimage on foot from Galatia to the tombs of the Holy Apostles in Rome, Alexandria, and Jerusalem in order to venerate and take [their] blessing, and he paid for these pilgrimages with his own means.

For our benefit he also told us this: "I never remember by mind ever departing from God."

C. On the mountain of Nitria, there is a tremendous church with a nearby lodging that is always able to accommodate any visiting stranger who wishes to stay, until he freely decides to leave. They let a guest stay for one week without having to work, and after this they give him work, whether in the garden, in bread-making, or in the kitchen, and they give him a book to read, not letting him meet with anyone until the sixth hour [noon]. Moreover, all the brothers make fabric with their own hands, so as to be self-sufficient.

II. From the Life of St. Euthymius

Euthymius the Great used to say to his disciples, "It is necessary for those who have abandoned their life [in the world] to attend always to obedience in their [new] life and to humble-mindedness. [They must take care] not to follow their own wills, always to be patient in every labor, both in arts and manual labor, especially for a man who is young and agitated by desire on account of his age. For then it is necessary for him to keep a greater watch over himself and to suppress the body with much hardship, in order for it be subject to reason, and for the flame of youth to be extinguished. And so as to become imitators of Paul and ones who fulfill his laws, let us not only avoid the accusation of slothfulness, since he judged the lazy and careless person unworthy even of nourishment, saying,

"He who is lazy, let him not eat." (cf. 2 Th 3:10), but also acquired goods with his own hands, saying, "These hands ministered to me and also to those with me" (cf. Acts 20:34; I Cor. 4:12).

For it would be most unusual for us not to give to others the fruit of our own hands, while the people in the world are able to provide for their wives, children, and their entire household, to pay the annual tax, to dedicate the first fruits of their labors to God, and to do as much good as they can.

III. From the Life of St. Sabbas the Sanctified

When our great Father Sabbas was young and staying in Flabianae, his hands were never negligent, but even when they were not stretched out toward God, prayer was the work he conducted at all times, lest the Enemy secretly sneak in unawares during even a brief cessation of his mental faculty. Hence the wings of virtue became lighter to him, and as to obedience, humility, and all the other evangelical virtues, he surpassed the whole brotherhood there, which was made up of about seventy brothers. Later, he departed from there with the knowledge and blessing of the Abbot and arrived at Jerusalem and there he met Euthymius the Great while he was proceeding to the *synaxis* as usual, and falling at his feet, Sabbas begged him with tears, supplicating him and refusing to leave so as to be made one of his rational sheep and to be shepherded by him alongside the others.

And indeed, the Great Euthymius was an excellent instructor who had himself gone through many such spiritual contests with much experience, and when he saw that Sabbas was still young, he feared that this desire might be owing only to a short-lived inclination, without being based in discretion of thoughts and the gravity that comes therefrom. [here: there's a play on the idea of weights]. Thus he did not allow him to live with the monks at the Lavra until he had passed his entire monastic training at the Coenobium and proved that he was capable of the required austerity.

Even after this Sabbas remained completely intransigent, and Euthymius said to him, "My child, you are too young to live at the Lavra. Being at the Lavra will neither bring you benefit, nor will it suit you. But if you will hear me, go now to the lower phrontistery, to Abba Theoktistos, for I know well that you will receive from him the greatest profit.

Once the blessed Sabbas had acceded to this (for among other things he was trained in obedience) and promised to do earnestly all that he had been commanded, he said, "This is what I desire, and for this reason I came to you for refuge, that I might be saved with your help." And so Euthymius sent Sabbas right away to the blessed Theoktistos, bidding him to give much guidance to him. For he said, knowing from insight, that he saw an abundant grace of the Spirit being poured out on Sabbas, and that it would not be long before his glory would fill the world. These things really did come to pass in the end, and Euthymius' prediction proved to be true.

Thus the divine Sabbas under the guidance of the blessed Theoktistos gave himself purely unto God and was possessed with a divine yearning. Moreover, seeing that his own constitution was twofold (I mean, made up of body and soul), he devised a twofold discipline. At one time he would engage in labors with the body, at another time in those of the soul, now spending the day in bodily labors, now passing the night in vigilant prayers; sometimes he would transport water, at other times he carried lumber, and as to the amount of work he did, he distinguished himself from all those who were assigned some service. Indeed he was possessed of a noble soul, and well-built in body and remarkably strong. Moreover, he took on other tasks by himself, even taking care of the mules. He was also the first to arrive to the Church *synaxis* and the last to depart, participating in the Divine Liturgy earnestly, and in all these things he invested obedience and moderation as his sacred capital. For this reason, he caused admiration among the assembly of monks, since they saw a crown of virtues and perfection adorning so young a man.

IV. From the Life of St. Lucian the Hieromartyr

When the Great Lucian was still young, he inclined towards the monastic life, and right from the beginning he fought against all pleasures of the flesh, standing fast in unceasing prayers and fasts; in short, he presented the flesh as subordinate to the spirit. He also practiced stenography, and by that means he provided food for himself and for the poor, since he considered it an injustice to partake of food himself before others had also partaken of his own livelihood.

V. From the Gerontikon

1. Once, Abba Ammoes and Abba Bitimios came to Abba Achillas very early in the morning, and they found him working making ropes. They asked for him to tell them a profitable word, and he said, "From the evening until now, I've woven forty yards of rope, and naturally I don't need all that, but [I fear] lest God be angry and condemn me, saying, 'Since you were capable of working, why did you not work?' For this reason I labor and use all my strength." And having been benefited, they departed.

2. Once, a brother came to Abba Silvanus on Mt. Sinai, and when he saw that the brothers were working, he told the elder, "Do not labor for the food that perishes. 'For Mary has chosen the good portion', as the Savior says. [Thus] the elder said to his disciple Zacharias, give this brother a book and put him in a cell without anything. And Zacharias did so. Therefore when the ninth hour came, the brother from a foreign country turned to the door, [to see] if they were going to call him to eat.

When no one called him, he rose and came to the Abba and said to him, "Abba, did the brothers not eat today?" But the elder said, "Of course." "Then why did you not call me?" And the elder answered, "Since you are a spiritual person and have no need for this food. But we are fleshly and want to eat, and that's why we work, whereas *you* have chosen the good portion, reading all day long and not wanting to eat fleshly food." And when he heard this, he prostrated, saying, "Forgive me, Abba." And the elder said, "In any case, Mary also needs Martha. For it is through Martha that Mary is praised."

3. There was a monk who was working on the feast day of a martyr, and when another monk saw him, he said to him, "Is it possible [for you] to be working today?" And he replied, "Today the servant of God was shattered and tortured in suffering martyrdom, and should I not exert myself just a little in my work?"

4. An elder was asked, "What must I do to be saved?" At that moment, the elder happened to be weaving a rope, and not lifting his head from the craft, he said, "Behold, as you see [me doing]."

5. Another elder came upon a river, and when he had found an area with reeds, he sat down, cut off some fibers and began weaving a rope on the riverbank, which he lowered into the river. He did so until people came and saw him, and then he rose and departed. He wasn't working because he had to, but for labor and silence.

6. One elder said, "When you arise in the morning, say to yourself, 'O body, work to be fed. O soul, be sober so as acquire your inheritance."

7. They said concerning Abba John the Dwarf that he had told his own elder brother when he was younger, "I want to be without cares, just like the Angels who have no worries, nor do they work, but worship God unceasingly." So he removed his garment and went into the desert, and after a week he came back to his brother. When he knocked on the door, his brother heard from inside and said before opening,
"Who are you?"
"It's me, your brother John."
But again his brother answered from within, "John has become an angel and no longer [dwells] among human beings."
But John begged him, saying, "It's me!"

In fact, he didn't open the door for him, but left him there to suffer until the morning. After this he opened the door and asked him, "Are you a human being? [Then] you have to start working again to be fed."

So John did a prostration before him and said, "Forgive me."

8. One elder said, "God has no desire for the slothful and lazy man."

VI. From St. Ephraim the Syrian[8]

Brother, do not neglect your craft; for oftentimes there comes a thought that suggests to you, "You'll never be able to learn this craft, since you're weak and incompetent. You can't bear the toil of this work for long. See how your limbs are beginning to suffer from this labor." And it says to you, "Since you can't get used to this toil, go back to where you came from. For you can be saved there too, if you wish to fear God."

Therefore do not be discouraged by such thoughts, but wait on the Lord who calls you to his Kingdom. For he says, "By your patience, gain your souls" (Lk 21:19). And also, "If you have faith like a grain of mustard seed you will say to this mountain, 'Move from here to there,' and it will move, and nothing will be impossible for you." So let us also be patient, beloved, for we have not put our hope in man who cannot save, but in God who saves them that hope in him.

So then, beloved, if you were learning to read and write, wouldn't you endure the stress? Or if you were learning a secular craft, wouldn't you endure the toil? And if you would endure these things with longsuffering, how much more ought we to endure all things for the Lord's sake? For it is written, "You shall eat the labors of your fruits.[9] Blessed are you, and it shall be well with you" (Ps 127:2 LXX). And the Apostle enjoins us, saying, "Doing honest labor with your own hands, not only

---

[8] Ephr.2.80D

[9] lit. tr. - not a typo

for your own nourishment, but also to give to the one in need out of your own labors" (cf. Eph 4:28). The person who hates working is a busybody, and indeed laziness causes much evil; but he who loves to work remains harmless.

Beloved brother, if you have chosen for yourself the life of piety[10], be sober lest through piety, the Evil One insinuate an alien thought, that is, a feeling of vainglory or pride, of not wanting to work together with your brothers, and to keep true piety from being destroyed; rather, work with them as if you were all of one soul, and thus preserve your piety. For slothfulness destroys piety, and it brings a shameful name to the one who has it. Therefore, combine your piety with earnestness and you shall be truly pious.

Beloved, if you are working at a *coenobium* and laboring for the rest of the brothers, see that the Evil One doesn't suggest to you a thought replete with the bitterness of death, and you say within yourself, "I'm missing out on any reward, and I don't have anything to eat," and so you seek more food, of a better quality than whatever the others are eating. Do not destroy the work of God for the sake of dirt. For if you set your heart on these things, you are no longer walking according to love. Besides, the one who seeks his reward from men, loses his reward from God.

So then, as long as you anticipate your reward from God, do not desire the rewards that come from men, but rather humble yourself before your brothers, and rejoice as you look to the retribution that comes from the Just Judge, who renders unto each according to his works, and who has said, "Who then is the faithful and wise servant whom his master has set over his household, to give them their food at the proper time? Blessed is that servant whom his master will find so doing when he comes. Truly, I say to you he will set him over all his possessions" (Mt 24:45-7).

I also know a brother who said, "I would pray to God to give grace to my craft, so that the whole *coenobium* would be benefited by it, since this would give me great joy and I would

---

[10] Trans. note: Εὐλάβεια, meaning attention, fear, respect can have the positive meaning of piety (εὐσέβεια), but also a negative meaning. Here it seems that Ephrem is warning about this potentially negative permutation of *piety*.

give yet more thanks to God who said, "Inasmuch as you have done it to one of the least of these my brethren, you have done it to me" (Mt 25:40).

And there was another brother who was working hard in the *coenobium*, and he was attacked by thoughts because of the work, but his response was to say to himself, "Ungrateful slave... Accept it: you have been sold and there is nothing else you can do." And God provided comfort to him.

Blessed is the monk who keeps the Lord's commandments and attends at all times to these three things: leisure at prayer, work, and study. For it is written, "Be still[11] and know that I am God" (Ps 45:11 LXX [46:10]), "I am poor and in toils from my youth" (Ps 87:16 LXX), and that the blessed man "shall meditate in His law by day and by night" (Ps 1:2 LXX).

Beloved, if you are in a *coenobium* of brothers, become humble-minded, being a servant to your brothers in everything, such that your way of life may instruct those who have come from a miserable life, and in seeing you they may raise up their own souls to the practice of the virtues. And so when those presiding at the monastery order the brothers to come together for work, go before the others eagerly, and do not wait for others to go before you, neither enter into competition with the heedless, who through their own carelessness greatly harm themselves and cause trouble, firstly because their disorderliness, self-love, and laziness brings judgment on them, secondly because they become deprived of the reward of labor, and thirdly, and most importantly, because they give others an excuse for murmuring, evil-speaking, and disobedience. Because they cause harm to others, they will receive the greater condemnation.

But as for you, brother, don't pay attention to these kinds of people. For at harvest time, no one ever says, "Because my neighbor isn't gathering wheat for himself, neither will I gather any for myself." But each person, in accordance with the season, gathers nourishment for himself and for his cattle, so that his needs are met in the wintertime. If then we show such

---

[11] This Greek phrase could also be translated, "Be at leisure."

care concerning things of the flesh, then how much more should we care about spiritual things? And in case your body is weak and cannot bear the toil like farmers do, then show your good intention with integrity, so that when others see your weakness and lack of strength, they may lift the burden from you. Do not allow them to take the burden from you altogether, but let them know, "I also wish to take part with you," and labor with them according to your strength which God has given you; and you shall have a great reward from God.

VII. From Abba Isaiah

Brother, for the sake of the Lord's commandment see that you do not neglect your craft, but attend to it in divine fear, lest you sin in your ignorance. Whatever craft it is you are being instructed in, ask the one who is showing you how to do it (and do not be ashamed to ask continually), "Do me a favor, could you look at this and tell me if it is good or not?"

If you are living with another brother and there is some additional work to do, do it yourself that you too might take part with your brother, and don't pity your body for the sake of an untroubled conscience. Moreover, never inquire into your brother's assignment, that is to see whether he works more than you, or you more than him. Force yourself to be attentive to your craft, and the fear of God will dwell with you. For laziness is the death and downfall of the soul.

VIII. From the Gerontikon

1. Once Abba Macarius the Great went to meet Abba Anthony on the mountain. When he knocked on the door, Abba Anthony came out and asked, "Who are you?" to which he replied, "I am Macarius." And as soon as Anthony heard that, he went inside, closed the door, and left him outside. After a long time had passed, he saw Macarius' patience, finally opened up to him, and joking he said, "I have long desired to see you, since I've heard so much about you!" He then showed

him hospitality and had some rest himself, since he had just finished much work.

When it was getting late, Abba Anthony began soaking some fibres for himself and Abba Macarius said, "Bid that I too may soak some for myself." "Here, take some," and taking them he began to cure a long stretch of cord. And so they sat weaving and speaking about the salvation of the soul until late in the evening, and the rope extended out through the door and down into the adjacent cave. When morning came, blessed Anthony entered the cave and, seeing the length of the rope that Abba Macarius had woven, he exclaimed, "Abundant strength comes forth from these hands!"

2. The heresy of the Messalians does not permit work. For it is necessary, they claim, to be engaged in pure prayer at all times; and so it teaches the hatred of work.

IX. From St. Ephraim

O monk, do not turn your weakness into an excuse out of sheer indolence, since it is written, "And the Lord gave them their desire" (cf. Ps 77:24-9 LXX). Brothers, let us not shun the grace of the Lord who provides us with strength to work the good. As we work the good by this strength, let us always give thanks to Christ. It is written, "Do not work for the good that perishes, but for the food that abides unto eternal life" (Jn 6:27). Let your hands work the good, so that the one in need may also have bread, and let your heart ever be turned toward the Lord, and then shall you be working for the food that abides, and not that which perishes. Therefore work and do not give yourself over to rest, that is do not walk in laziness. For laziness has proved to cause abundant evil.

Principle 4
What purpose the monk must work for;
what manner of works he should perform, and for how much time.

I. From the Gerontikon

1. Once some brothers went to a great elder; when they arrived, he asked the first brother, "What work do you do, brother?" and he answered, "I weave ropes, Abba." The elder said to him, "God shall weave a crown for you, my child."

He asked the second brother, "What work do you do?" and he answered, "Reeds." And the elder said to him, "God shall strengthen you, my child."

He then asked the third brother, "And you, what work do you do?" He answered, "I make sieves." "God shall protect you, my child."

He asked the fourth brother, "What work do you do?" He replied, "I am a calligrapher." He simply said, "You understand."

Then, when he asked the fifth brother, "What work do you do?" and he answered, "I weave fine linens." And the elder said, "I have no business saying anything about that."

The elder then proceeded to make clear all that he had said: "He who weaves ropes, as long as he keeps sobriety in his thoughts, weaves for himself a crown from God. Whoever works among the reeds is in need of strength, for that requires much labor. Anyone who makes sieves needs protection from God, because he goes to the cities to sell them. Now, a calligrapher needs to humble his own heart, because this craft brings arrogance to those who are not attentive. And to one who weaves fine linens, I have nothing to say, since he is doing business, not performing a monastic labor. For if someone from afar sees a man carrying baskets or reeds or sieves, he thinks, "That must be a monk." For the monk's handicraft is grass, and it goes into the fire to be burnt. But if someone sees a man selling textiles, he says, "Look, merchants have come." For this craft is of the world, and it is not spiritually beneficial for people especially not for monks.

2. When he was young, Abba John the Eunuch asked an elder, "How is it that you were all able to do the work of God while in a state of rest, while we are unable to do this work even with much labor?" The elder replied, "We were able because we held God's work to be of primary importance, and we gave the least significance to bodily needs; on the other hand, you consider bodily needs to be most important, giving the work of God much less significance, and this is why you exhaust yourselves, since you do not consider what the Savior said to his disciples, "Seek first the Kingdom of God, and all these things will be added to you" (cf. Mt 6:33).

3. A brother once asked an elder, "What should I do, since I am displeased with my handicraft? For I love to make ropes, but I'm unable to do that job." And the elder said, "Abba Sisoes used to say that we shouldn't do work that makes us content."

4. A brother asked Abba Biare, "What shall I do to be saved?" The elder replied, "Go, make your belly small, your labor little, do not become agitated in your cell, and you will be saved. That is, conduct your life in self-control, contentment with little, and without anxiety.

II. From St. Ephraim the Syrian

Brother, be strictly attentive to yourself, for the malevolence of the Enemy is much and manifold, and he makes use of various devices. For at times the Deceiver suggests to you slothfulness at your work, and through despondency he fights to keep you away from work, whether by making you treat what isn't work as if it were, or by getting you to leave your cell to dawdle about without any reason, while abandoning your usual assignment. But if you make a stand against him through patience and attentiveness, he will wage war against you with a different method. He'll give you an eagerness to work that is more than what is necessary, motivated by passion, whether it be greed or the love of material things, and to this end he will strengthen you to get up early and stay up till late, so that if possible he may even deter you from prayer and church. When you are summoned for liturgy, he persuades you to arrive last of all and induces you to depart before everyone else at the dismissal of liturgy, all through an excessive concern for your work. And in this way he lords over you by degrees, until he gets you to be altogether materialistic and earthly. "For whatever overcomes a person, to that he is enslaved," (2 Pet 2:19) says the Scripture.

Since then you know the deceit of the Enemy, beloved, do not submit to him, but do all things in the measure proper to them, and work in moderation so that you may have leisure at prayer and liturgy; and the prayer of faith will give you strength and grace for every good work. Let us walk in self-sufficiency and be eager [to obtain] necessities, not amenities. When we go after amenities and acquisitions, the toil is great, the road treacherous, the trouble uncompensated, and life full of worries, while there is need for one thing only, my brothers, as the Lord says (cf. Lk 10:41-2). There is nothing higher or more honorable than the soul, and for its sake let us run, showing care and earnestness, rather than spending all our time on the care of the body.

So whenever our body hungers and demands nourishment, let us remind ourselves that the soul is seeking out its own needs, as well. Just as the body is unable to live if it does not partake of food, so too the soul, if it does partake of spiritual wisdom, is dead. Hence the Lord said, "Man shall not live by bread alone (Mt. 4:4; Lk. 4:4; Deu. 8:3). So then may you, as a good steward, give the food of the soul to the soul and that of the body to the body, and don't let your own soul be mortified, but nourish it with words divine, "in psalms and hymns and spiritual songs" (Eph 5:19; cf. Col 3:16); with readings from the divine Scriptures, with fasts, vigils, and tears; with hope and meditation on the good things to come.

These things and the like are nourishment and life for the soul. Brothers, see to it that none of you is found to be without fruit, for the Apostle says, "Whatever one sows, that will he also reap" (Gal 6:7). Thus, the one who sows luxury, pleasures, and ease to the flesh, will reap from the flesh corruption. But the one who sows to the spirit prayer, fasting, and vigil, will reap from the spirit eternal life. He who does not remain set on the same assignment will be overwhelmed by unprofitable works [and distractions]. An inconstant man works on holy days and dawdles on workdays. But to behave dishonorably and insensibly, this is no virtue; rather, one should have understanding and reject carelessness. For as the [Proverb] says, "The sluggard is not ashamed when he is reproached" (Pro 20:4 LXX).

III. From the Canons of the Apostles

As soon as they rise in the morning, let every faithful man and woman pray after they have first washed themselves. And if any homily of spiritual instruction is being given, let them prefer that to their work.

Principle 5
What [rule] brothers ought to keep when they work with one another.

I. From Abba Isaiah

1. Brothers, whenever you go to do a task with each other, let each one of you be attentive to yourself and not to your brother, looking to see who's working more than the other. Moreover, do not teach and order another around, even if you happen to see him doing something wrong. Do not say, "You've ruined it!" but rather let him do the work as he likes. If, however, someone says, "Do me a favor, teach me this," then teach him in humility. If, even though you know how to do it, you say you don't know how and refuse to teach your brother, you do not have the love of God in yourself, but possess wickedness. Let the one who does not know how to do the work not be ashamed to ask continually of him who knows, "Do me a favor, tell me if this is alright."

2. If, while you work with each other, someone botches up the work out of timidity, let no one chastise him, but rather be cheerful toward him.

3. If you are working with someone sickly or infirm, do not be competitive, wishing to outdo him.

4. When you are doing your work, make an effort not to examine what you have accomplished or what your brother accomplished that week; that would not be progress, but regress.

5. When you go off to do a task with your brother, do not make it your desire that others learn how you have accomplished more than him; for what God seeks from man is this: to do each work in secret (cf. Mt 6:1-18).

6. When you are doing work with others, do not bear [in mind] any fault that you see or hear while you are among

others, lest it be found on your tongue when you are speaking with your brothers; for this is death for the soul, even if you be wise.

II. From Abba Cassian

In all the cenobitic monasteries in the East, especially in Egypt, this sort of rule is kept: at the time of the dismissal of the liturgy none of the brothers dares stand and talk with anyone else. Neither [is it permitted] for any of them to go out of their cell or to abandon the work they have in hand, in fulfilment of the apostolic injunction[12], unless there is some necessity, and [in that case] they all gather together for the completion of some necessary work, and this they do carefully and silently, so that no conversation begins between them, but each one conducts his assigned task while remaining focused on the psalm and study. They take great care that none of the brothers ever remains behind with another, especially with a novice, and that none of them ever dares stretch out his hands to hold or embrace another; if anyone is found transgressing this rule, he is given the most severe punishment.

---

[12] cf. 1 Th 2:9

Principle 6
That in the cenobitic monastery one should not acquire any property of his own,
and there is a risk of the severest punishment for one who is acquisitive

I. From Gregory the Dialogist

There was a monk by the name of Justus who had studied medicine. While I was still at the monastery where he lived, he used to help treat the usual (* illnesses I am prone to suffer. He was stricken with a bodily illness and in his last days. His brother according to the flesh, whose name is Copiosus, used to come to him and wait on him in his illness; as a matter of fact, he still lives nearby, providing income for himself in this temporary life by practicing medicine in the city.

When the sick man perceived that he was nearing death, he revealed to his brother Copiosus that he had hidden away gold coins. The brothers of the monastery searched thoroughly all that remained in his infirmary and found the three gold pieces there, and right away they informed me. When I learned of this evil concerning a brother who was living among us, I couldn't bear it; for our monastery's rule was such that all the brothers were to live in common and no one would acquire anything only for himself. And so I was stricken with grief, and I meditated how I might do something beneficial, both for the purification of the dying man and to establish a spirit of fear and correction among the brothers who were living.

So I called on the steward of the Monastery and said to him, "Go and tell the brothers not to approach the dying man, and that he can't hear any word of consolation from the mouth of any of the brothers. But if when he is about to die, he calls on the brothers, let his brother in the world say to him that it is on account of the three coins that he hid that he has been shunned by all the brothers. For perhaps at his death he will at least condemn his own heart in bitter remorse for this fault and somehow be cleansed of sin. And when he passes away, do not bury his body where the rest of the brothers are buried, but

59

make a sort of hole in the dung and throw his body in there, and let the three coins that he left behind be cast on top of him. Then let all the brothers cry out together, 'Let your money perish together with you,' and cover him with earth."

It came to pass that as Justus was at the point of death and was greatly afflicted, he sought to present himself to the brothers. However, when none of the monks came to him, his genuine brother informed him why he had been spurned by all. At that moment, he sighed deeply for his sin, and with this sigh he departed from the body and then was buried as I had ordered.

All the brothers were then terribly distraught by the lot that was given to Justus, and each of them began to bring forward trifles and the smallest things which the rule of the coenobium had forbidden, greatly fearing that something would be discovered by the others [eventually] which would bring about the same condemnation.

After his death, when thirty days had already passed, I began to pity the deceased brother in my soul and to consider his judgment with the deepest pain, and so I decided to seek out some plan for his redemption. Once again I called upon the steward and with much grief I told him, "The deceased brother has been disregarded by us for long enough now, and now we are obliged by love to do whatever we can to help him. Go then, and from today onward, offer the bloodless sacrifice unceasingly on his behalf every day until thirty days have been completed." And the steward did as he was told.

It came to pass that the saving sacrifice was offered on his behalf as I have said, and being occupied with other matters we did not keep track of the number of days that had passed when that brother who had died appeared at night to his relative, Copiosus, while he was asleep. Upon seeing him, he asked him, "What kind of [spirits] are you among there, brother?" And he answered, "Until now I was in a really bad state, but now I am well." Copiosus went to the monastery right away and made this known to us, and when we had accurately counted the number of days, we learned that on that very day was completed the thirtieth offering on behalf of the departed brother, Justus.

2. From the Gerontikon

1. A brother once asked Abba Poemen, "I wish to come and live at the coenobium. And the elder replied, "If you wish to come to the coenobium, [you must know that] so long as you do not put aside your anxiety concerning all circumstances and matters, you will be unable to work at the coenobium. For there you will not even have control over the water jar."

2. Abba Poemen's brother, Paisios, once found a vessel full of denarii, and he said to his [other] brother Abba Anoub, "You see that the word that Abba Poemen teaches is quite harsh; come then, let us go build a monastery for ourselves somewhere, and let's live there without any cares. Abba Anoub asked him, "How will we get the resources to build?" So he showed him the denarii, and when Abba Anoub saw them, he was deeply grieved as he considered the harm that would come to his brother's soul from this. He said to him, "Let us go and build a cell beyond the river." Then he took the vessel and tucked it away in his cloak, and as they were passing the river and were halfway to the other side, and then Abba Anoub made it look like his cloak along with the coins fell out by accident, as he was turning around. They were lost in the river, and Abba Anoub pretended to feel bad about what had happened. But Paisios said to him, "Do not feel bad, Abba; since the denarii have gone, let's go back to our brother." So they returned and lived in peace.

3. An elder said, "Many monks have cast aside their wealth and abandoned both father and mother, siblings and relatives, on account of their own sins; nevertheless, after coming to the Coenobium and [even] accomplishing great virtues, they have been led astray by the smallest trifles and have become the laughing stock of demons by surrounding themselves with leather bags and chests containing fruits and snacks, needles and scissors, and knives and belts. Such people are rightly considered and reproved as lovers of self, and as cursed to the outer darkness, in accordance with Divine Scripture. For it says

that whoever alters the definitions of the Fathers is accursed. [Moreover], as initiates and participants together with Ananias, Sapphira, and Jannes, they will deserve the same lot that befell them (Acts 5:1-11; 2 Tim 3:8)."

2. From the Gerontikon

He who enters a Coenobium to live the monastic life and [yet] retains any of his [old] possessions will not be able to remain under the subjection and guidance of the monastery for long, neither will he be able to achieve the virtue of humility and obedience, or endure the poverty of the cenobitic way of life to the end. For when some pretext or grievance kindles his imagination, the hope he has invested in the property he has left behind will quickly cast him out of the monastery, like a stone from a slingshot. The rebellions of the other passions, I mean anger and desire, seem to have their causes in the body, and in some ways they are innate, beginning at birth, and only over a long period of time are they overcome. The disease of greed, on the other hand, striking from without, is easier to prevent as long as [you have] caution and prayer. However, if it remains untreated, it becomes more destructive than the other passions, and more difficult to get rid of. "For the love of money is the root of all kinds of evils," (1 Tim 6:10) according to the Apostle.

So then, when this disease finds a soul that is very lukewarm and unbelieving at the beginning of obedience, it suggests to that person "just rewards" and excuses that seem good and reasonable, with the aim of getting him to keep a portion of what he formerly possessed. For it fixes in the mind of the monk [a concern about] old age and bodily weakness, and [the thought] that the necessities provided by the monastery are not sufficient for consolation, either for a sick man or a healthy one; and then from there [the thought arises] that neither is there proper care for the sick monks, and [they] are neglected. And therefore, if he does not have gold hidden away, he will [surely] die miserably. Finally, it persuades him that he will be unable to live his entire life at the monastery because of the burden of his duties and the strictness of the abbot.

And when, by these sorts of impressions, [this passion] deceives the miserable man into storing away just a single denarius, it then proceeds to persuade him to learn some trade without the knowledge of the abbot, by which he'll be able to increase his cherished money. Eventually, it deludes the wretch with unsure hopes, enticing him with the profit, comfort, and freedom from anxiety that he'll get from his trade; and once he is completely bound by the thought of this gain, he does not consider either of the contraries that might befall him, [that is] either the madness of anger if he happens to suffer any loss, or the darkness of sorrow if he fails to acquire the gain he had hoped for. And just as the belly has become a god to others, gold becomes a god to him, and so he becomes an idol-worshipper, according to the judgment of the Apostle (cf. Ph 3:19; Col 3:5). For as soon as his mind has been estranged from the love of God, he [begins to] love men's idols, sculpted with gold.

A monk's mind is darkened by these thoughts, and as his condition becomes worse, he is unable to preserve any humility or obedience, but grows resentful and again breaks out with passion. At each of his assignments he grumbles and complains, and once he ceases to keep any commandment or sense of piety, he becomes like a wild horse hurdling towards a precipice, and is no longer content with his daily food. And he protests that he can't bear these things his whole life, and says, "It's not as if God is in this place only, neither is my own salvation confined to this place, but he is he be found anywhere that people seek him out," [drawing the conclusion that] if he doesn't get out of that monastery, he'll perish. And so this corrupt mindset, along with the money he stored up as an aid, become as it were wings to him, and he plans his flight from the monastery. Then, in response to all the instructions given him at the monastery he reacts proudly and harshly, considering himself someone who does not really belong there, and a stranger to the monastery.

When he sees anything in need of improvement, he fails to care for it [himself, but] regards it with contempt; he criticizes everything that goes on at the monastery, since he is searching for excuses to get angry and upset, so that it doesn't seem like he is removing himself from the guidance of the coenobium lightly or without good reason. And if he is able to deceive someone else with whispers and vain words into abandoning the monastery, he will do that too, since he wishes to have an accomplice with this same fault of his; this is how enflamed he is with the fire of his own possessions, and he will never be able to find peace at the monastery or live under a rule.

When the devil, like a wolf, lays hold of him and snatches him away from the flock, and is getting ready to devour him, he then get him to do the following: the works that he has been neglecting to do at the assigned work hours of the Coenobium, these he does with great enthusiasm in his own cell, day and night. And the devil does not suffer him to keep either the customary hours of prayer, or the rule of fasting, or the canon of vigils, but having ensnared him with the madness of greed, he convinces him to give all his attention to his trade.

Moreover, there are three forms of this disease, all of which are forbidden by the divine Scriptures and the teachings of the Fathers. First then, there is that one form which we have outlined above, which gets pitiful men to acquire and treasure things that they didn't even have in the world; second, there is a form that causes others to regret that they have renounced once and for all their possessions, and it incites them to take back what they have [already] offered to God. The third form enfolds the monk with unbelief and lukewarmness from the beginning, and it doesn't allow him to be entirely released from the things of the world, but suggests that he should keep something out of fear of poverty, as we said before, and from lack of faith in God's providence; [and thus the passion] proves him to be a transgressor of those promises he himself made when he renounced the world.

Examples of each of these three forms are described in Divine Scripture, and we have found them to be condemned there. For Gehazi, wishing to acquire wealth that he did not formerly have, failed to attain the grace of prophecy that his teacher wished to leave to him in the way of inheritance, and instead of a blessing he inherited an eternal leprosy [that he would pass on to all of his offspring] through the curse of the Prophet Elisha (2 Ki 5:15-27 [4 Ki LXX]). Then, Judas wished to acquire money which he had formerly given up to follow Christ, and not only did his sickness [of soul develop to the point] that he betrayed the Master and so fell from the Choir of the Apostles, but even in the flesh his life was ended by a violent death. Lastly, Ananias and Sapphira, when they kept a part of what they possessed, were punished with death by the mouth of the Apostle Peter.

And indeed, through Moses in Deuteronomy, God mystically gives a command to those who, despite having promised to renounce the world, cling again to earthly things through the cowardice of disbelief, saying, "Anyone who is much afraid and is cowardly in his heart shall not go out into battle; let him go and be dismissed to his own home, lest he instill fear in his brothers' hearts" (cf. Deut 20:8). In saying these things, he instructs us who have renounced the world to do so completely, and thus to *go into battle*, and not to detract others from the perfection of the Gospel by making a mean and spoiled beginning ourselves, putting cowardice in others' hearts. Perhaps also relevant to us is that word which Basil the Great said to a certain senator who had made a lukewarm renunciation of the world and kept some of his own wealth: "You lost your senatorship, and yet you never even became a monk."

Therefore it is necessary for us to cut off from our own souls the love of money, which is the root of all kinds of evils, knowing with certainty that as long as the root remains, the shoots will quickly sprout up. We ought to have before our eyes the uncertainty of death, since perhaps the Lord will come at an hour we do not expect, and will find us with our conscience corrupted by the love of money, and will say to us what was said in the Gospel to that rich man, "Fool! This night your soul is required of you, and the things you have prepared whose will they be?" (Lk 12:20).

Moreover, it is necessary to know that it is difficult to attain this virtue if one does not live in a coenobium, because in a cenobitic community we have freedom from anxiety when it comes to these sorts of needs.

Principle 7

That anyone who steals or removes any of the various things that belong to the monastery sins gravely against God, and shall receive a greater punishment.

Thus, it is necessary to take great care for such things, as being dedicated to God, and not to disdain the least of them; and that negligence in regard to all such things is injurious.

I. From the Life of St. Euthymius

1. There was a monk from Galatia named Theodotus, who was a brother at the monastery of St. Euthymius. By a plot of the Evil One, the following event took place. Stephen, who was the abbot of the monastery before Thomas, had inherited six hundred gold pieces from his brother's fortune when he passed away, and Stephen dedicated them to the monastery. The money was being kept in the deacons' quarters, and unbeknownst to Thomas of Apamea, to whom was entrusted the care of the monastery, Theodotus stole it. When he arose early in the morning he pretended to be upset and extremely agitated, as if he could not enjoy any peace and quiet, and thence he departed from the monastery under the pretense that he desired a place free of noise, but in reality he was just making haste to disappear with the gold.

While rushing on his way to the Holy City, he passed by a place across from the Monastery of the Monk Martyrios, and there he sat down and rested. He decided to set apart fifty of the gold pieces he had stolen, and the rest he placed under a large stone, and as soon as he marked the place, he continued his journey to Jerusalem. From Jerusalem he went to Joppa and rented some horses by leaving a deposit, and then returned to the stone under which he hid the gold. When he was already near the place, O the eyes of God that see all things! O most just of judgments! Theodotus beheld a serpent slithering from the stone, massive in size and terrible to look upon, just as if it were ordered to guard the gold pieces and attempting to keep Theodotus away from what belonged to someone else. Terrified at the sight, he left empty-handed, and came back down at a later time only to find that same dreadful guard keeping careful watch over the gold, and as it were keeping vigil. Not only did it not let him approach to take the money from underneath the stone, but it struck at him fiercely, and he was happy simply to get away from there unharmed.

Once again, at a later time, Theodotus came near the place, when suddenly an airborne power flew down upon him and just like a club it struck him down, inflicting on him a mortal wound, flipping him over, and leaving him for dead on the ground. Yet, some Lazariotes were on duty in the area and when they found him deserted in this miserable state, they took him up and brought him to a hospital near the Holy City. After he had been laying there for much time, in a dream he beheld an old man who looked indignant and said, "There is no other way I can revive you unless you give back the money that was stolen from the Monastery of Euthymius."

Thereupon he sent for the overseer from his bed and revealed to him the theft he had committed, and all else that had occurred, and he requested that he report all of this to the monastery. And as soon as the attendants of the Abbot Thomas and Leontius learned of what happened, they went straight to the Holy City and placed Theodotus on a stretcher so that he could show them the place where he had hidden the gold. And thus did they find it under the stone, and as for that dreadful guard, the serpent, what a wonder! it was nowhere to be found, having withdrawn for the sake of the true owners of the treasure. After they had retrieved the gold, they returned directly to the monastery, considering the amount spent by Theodotus to be of little account, and Theodotus himself became safe from all harm and recovered his bodily health.

2. There was also another man, a Cilician by origin, a monk by *schema*, whose name was Paul. He was driven out of the Monastery of Martyrios since he had been possessed by an evil spirit, and then he was brought by his companions to the tomb of Euthymius. When he was placed by the reliquary and some time had passed, the Great Saint appeared to him around

midnight and drove away the demon. And the truth of the report of this healing is indisputable because that very night Paul left from the tomb at the time of the midnight vigil and went to chant with the choir, and he then testified about this healing before us all. And I, the author, was already a member of the monastery of the Great Saint at that time.

Paul continued to remain at the coenobium all his life, preserving in his heart gratitude for this miracle, and he earnestly took part in all the labor and tasks along with the other brothers. Once, while we were together with Paul, gathering from the desert a nutritious plant that we have the habit of calling *manuthia*, we asked him what he had been through, how he had come to the coenobium, and how he had come to experience that miraculous healing. Since he felt a sense of familiarity with us, he explained everything clearly and in detail.

And so he began to recount his story, saying, "I was trusted with a service at the Monastery of Martyrius, and I really don't know how I was so taken by the passion of greed… Because I was poor and had no means to make even a single drachma, the thought occurred to me to steal some of the holy vessels and so provide myself with some property. Then, once I was conquered by this wicked thought and I had cast from myself the fear of God, I removed the keys from the altar, opened the storage for the holy vessels; I wickedly appropriated most of them for myself, and gave a few away to others. After this, and upon completion of my service, I placed the keys back on the altar, and afterwards I went to have supper with some of the brothers, drank my fill of wine, and then laid down on my bed in misery. At that point all kinds of indulgent thoughts poured into my soul, and everything seemed to be making [my condition] worse; since my imagination was still corrupted by drunkenness, I gladly gave myself over to these passions, and they so consumed me that they even set me to hallucinating that I was next to a woman, sleeping with her.

"Then suddenly a dark and dismal cloud came upon me, out of which there came an unclean demon that rushed upon me, and I was overpowered. I remained captive to it and was often tormented by it, and what evils did I not then suffer? When was this enemy ever satiated with evil doing, as soon as he was granted power to do evil through me? And this continued until the brothers took pity on me and carried me to the reliquary of the saint. When I was placed there, I somehow came to myself and with warm tears I beseeched the saint to take pity on me and deliver me from the influence of this evil demon. I persisted in my supplication that whole night, and I was not found wanting when I left from there.

"Suddenly, in the dead of night, I appeared to be in a place wondrous and divine; everyone would long to see its ambiance, its beauty and grace, and nobody would be able to describe it with words. However, it seemed that upon my own head there was a black cloak, made of wool. -- O Euthymius, thou servant of God that wardest off all evil, may this cloak be kept far hence! -- For inside it bore thorns instead of wool, and these were not small, nor could they be moved, but in size and shape they were similar to the points used for writing instruments. They pricked my head with such intensity that I could hardly breathe.

"Tortured by this evil thing, I remember turning to Euthymius and calling his name, and straightway he appeared to me, illuminated by a halo of abundant light! His hair was grey, his face round, and his eyes were shining. He was short in stature, with a low-hanging beard, and he was wrapped in a black mantle with a staff in hand; then he approached me and said, "What do you want me to do for you?"

In fear and trembling I answered, "Take pity on me in my suffering, and deliver me from this evil demon!" He then looked at me more sternly, and said, "Have you now been convinced that nothing that is done can be hidden from God? Have you learned from what you suffered just how great an evil it is for one to despise what is God's, especially what has been consecrated to him? For just as the eucharistic offering in all the churches goes directly up to God, he in turn knowing to provide his gifts from above, so too those that misuse such things transgress against none other than God himself, and suffer a just judgment.

Indeed, if Ananias and his wife received punishment for taking back what they themselves had offered to God, so that they even suffered death because of the theft, what kind of pardon will there be for someone who has not even spared the offerings of others? That is, unless you give a promise that you will no longer lay your unjust hands on holy things, and that you will not indulge in the acceptance of wicked thoughts." And the saint stated, "[If you promise this, then] God will certainly heal you, for he is the Friend of Man and, as the Divine Prophecies teach, 'he does not desire the death of the sinner, but that he should convert and live' (Ez 18:23). So then, this is how the present torments came to you; when you were entrusted with the ministry of the Holy Things, you did not remain faithful to God, but immediately you turned to deceit and theft, 'reaping where you did not sow, and gathering where you did not scatter,' as is rightly said.[13] From these evil actions there came about the passions of perversion and immoderation, and consequently, this terrible influence of demons."

After hearing these words of the saint, I made a promise that was to be kept for my whole life. He then looked upon the unclean demon with wrath and grasped at the cloak with his hand, and as soon as he had powerfully thrust it from my head, its appearance immediately changed and in the hand of the saint it looked like a tiny Ethiopian, but with eyes like fire. The saint then dug what seemed to be a terribly deep pit, and he let the demon escape into it. He turned again to me and said what Christ had said to the paralytic, "Behold, you have become well. Sin no more that nothing worse may happen to you" (Jn 5:14). Released from this passion I gave fervent thanks to God; and ever since being free of that passion, I have been preserved from all such evils.

The author adds: Paul related these facts to me, and here I publish the account for the benefit of all.

II. From Abba Cassian

---

[13] This clearly has echoes of NT language, but I don't think it's meant as a verse quotation. Besides, Euthym. uses the less common quotation formula, ἀληθῶς ειπεῖν

Throughout the cenobitic communities of the East, they do rotations nearly every week both at the kitchens and at other services, the purpose being both to rest [from certain tasks] as well as simply to fulfill [the commandment] of love by working for others. At the completion of each weekly rotation, after the morning prayers on the Lord's Day, they hand over the designated tools for the use of the brothers coming to take their place, and these in turn, when they receive them, are earnest to show care and attention for the tools and vessels, to keep them from being broken or damaged, so much so that they treat them like sacred vessels consecrated to God. They prepare themselves not only as accountable to the monastery steward who is present, but as accountable to God, if anything happens to be broken or damaged due to their negligence or carelessness. And to demonstrate what I am saying, I will add to the account exactly what we saw with our own eyes.

At one point during one of the weeks, the steward who was present saw a brother spilling a few lentils on the ground. This he did not overlook as some trivial matter, but he held it against the brother and gave him a penalty, since having been given a responsibility for that week, he had treated things dedicated to God with negligence and had trampled on his own conscience in doing so. For they organize and care for everything with such faithfulness and attentiveness that even those things that seem to us slight and trivial, these they give much attention. For instance, they would reposition a jar that has been wrongly placed, or clean up the spill from a dish, believing that even for these sorts of things they will receive a reward from the Lord God.

Throughout all the East these weekly rules are maintained, as I said, except for in Egypt. Among the Egyptians, the monks do not shift their obedience's at all, but everyone remains at the same assignment where he has been tested, and which has proved to be suited to him, for as long as he is able, and so long as neither old age nor illness prevent him. Thus, the management of the kitchen will be granted to a brother who is the most experienced of all of those [that work in the kitchen], as long as his strength of body serves him and he is continuing to make progress in virtue.

III. From St. Ephraim

1. Negligence is the betrayer of all that is good, and it is succeeded by a terrible captivity that involves not only slothfulness in one's handiwork, but also disorganization in one's own life. However, he who abides in this state can flee from it when he wills to do so.

2. A slothful monk does not even close the front door of his cell until it creaks from being battered by the wind; but the diligent monk is beyond reproach.

Principle 8
With what manner of disposition one ought to serve (or be served),
and what kind of spiritual profit comes from service.

I. From Antiochus of Palestine[14]

He who serves at the monastery ought to do so diligently, with all his strength, knowing that the work he does is the work of God, and thus he should not be negligent in anything, whether by reason of sluggishness, or dejection, or irritation, or due to conflict with certain brothers. For everything in the monastery is dedicated to God, and he who serves carelessly is subject to the gravest danger, since in so doing he despises God himself, for "inasmuch as you have done it to one of the least of these my brothers, you have done it to me," and again, "inasmuch as you did not do it to one of the least of these, you have not done it to me" (Mt 25:40). So then, whether one serves diligently or negligently, his service is rendered to God above.

Hear then what the Prophet Jeremiah says concerning those who serve negligently: "Cursed is the man who does the work of the Lord negligently" (Jer 48:10 [31:10 LXX]). Let us strive not to fall under this dreadful curse, brothers, but as servants of Christ let us fulfill our service with all due diligence and attention, that we may also partake of the blessing, as disciples of the Blessed One who said, "If anyone serves me, let him follow me, and where I am, there shall also my servant be; if anyone serves me, the Father will honor him. (Jn 12:28)." And elsewhere, *I am among you as one who serves, for* "the Son of Man came not to be served but to serve, and to give his life as a ransom for many" (Mt 20:28). He enjoins much the same when he says to his disciples, "If anyone would be first, he must be last of all and servant of all" (Mk 9:35).

Moreover, let us hearken to what the Apostle says, "Behold, now is the favorable time. Behold, now is the day of

---
[14] Author of the Pandects.

salvation. We put no obstacle in anyone's way, so that no fault may be found with our ministry, but as servants of God we commend ourselves in every way: by great endurance in afflictions, hardships, calamities, in beatings, imprisonments, riots, labors, vigils, hunger; by purity, knowledge, patience, kindness, the Holy Spirit, genuine love, truthful speech" (2 Cor 6:2-7), "as bondservants of Christ, doing the will of God from the soul, rendering service with a good will, as to the Lord and not to men" (Eph 6:6-7). And he again exhorts us, saying, "Therefore, my beloved brethren, be steadfast, immovable, always abounding in the work of the Lord, knowing that in the Lord your labor is not in vain" (1 Cor 15:58). "For God is not unjust so as to overlook your work and the love that you have shown for his name in serving the saints, as you still do" (Heb 6:10). The Apostle Paul also says of himself, "At present I am going to Jerusalem to minister to the saints" (Rom 15:25), and he beseeches the brethren, "strive together with me in your prayers to God on my behalf, that I may be delivered from the unbelievers in Judah and that my service for Jerusalem may be acceptable to the saints" (Rom 15:30-31).

Therefore, brothers, let us consider how these beacons of the world and pillars of the Church ministered to the poor in Jerusalem with such zeal and effort, and how much more we are obliged to minister to our brothers in the Lord earnestly and attentively, and to strive in every way to serve others, as serving God through them.

II. From St. Barsanuphius

1. A brother once went to an elder for counsel, saying, "I fall down before you, compassionate father, that I might be strengthened by your prayers, for I perceive that all my day is spent in distraction, and I hardly have any time for the remembrance of God. Further, whenever God does provide me with a little sorrow for my errors, by your prayers, I gradually lose it because of new distractions from outside. I also worry about my management of the infirmary, that as a position of authority it will make me more talkative and arrogant, or that it

will probably lead me into gluttony because I am constantly handling food for meals. And understand, father, that I am saying these things not because I feel despondency or boredom in my service. What should I do then, wretched that I am? I'm afraid that, if I remain at this task, I will nourish these passions of mine, that is, either due to my own [weak will] or due to the influence of demons. But do you, father, make clear to me the will of God; and strengthen me by your prayers that I might do what you say, and grant me forgiveness."

The elder answered, "Hear, brother, and understand with the help of the Lord that from the moment we granted you to embark on this task, our heart and guiding hand have been with you, or rather, the hand of God is with you. We beseech him in prayer for the salvation of your soul, and to strengthen you in this matter, and for his good favor and protection; and in this manner will you be saved, not in any other way. Therefore do not grow despondent, but when you fall, get back up, and when you make mistakes, blame yourself, until the Lord provides to you the mercy that you desire.

"Take care that you are not negligent. And concerning distraction, brother, let me say this: many people have heard about a city, and then, when they happen to enter it, they do not even realize that they are *in* the city. And you, do you not realize that you are abiding in the remembrance of God all day long? You see, being given a commandment and dedicated to keeping it, this is both obedience to God and remembrance of him. And Brother John was right in telling you, 'Put forth the leaves, and by the will of God you will also bear the fruits.' And when you do not know what is beneficial, go to those that do know; this is humility, and in this way you will find the grace of God.

"Know, then, that this is salvation for you. For your coming here did not happen apart from God, but he led you here. Be strengthened in the Lord, for there is no small gain to be borne from bearing this sort of distraction that you describe. Moreover, since we have not yet attained to perfection, so as to be completely freed from the captivity of the passions, it is more profitable to converse amidst the distraction of your service than to converse with the passions. So be confident that the

Lord is the one who has placed you in this work, and that he will provide, and that we also bear with you the burden of this responsibility. Do not let the devil deceive you with rationalizations, for it is said that "by reasonable sounding words they deceive the hearts of the innocent" (Rom 16:18). But he who set you on this way, he is all that matters: the one who said to his disciples, "Behold I send you forth" (Mt 10:16) and, "Behold, I am with you" (Mt 28:20). Fear not, and do not be remiss in anything concerning the infirmary, growing despondent from the cares of this responsibility. If you bring to mind what I have told you, you will not have a problem. Only, you ought to give heed to yourself according to your strength,[15] and God will come to your aid; be strengthened in him.

2. There was another brother who was assigned gatekeeping at the coenobium and was getting exhausted because of working by himself. He asked the same great elder whether he should take on another brother to help him or not. The elder replied, "Brother, if anyone wishes to come to the Lord and to walk the path of salvation, he should learn to anticipate temptations, afflictions, and pains at each and every hour. For the Scripture says, "Son, if you come to serve the Lord, prepare your soul for temptations" (Sir 2.1). And the Lord said, "If anyone wishes to follow me, let him deny himself and take up his cross daily and follow me" (Lk 9:23). Therefore, he who wishes to become his disciple must be obedient till death.

It will be more beneficial for you to be alone and not to labor overmuch, rather than having someone else with you [at all times]. If however there ever arises some need, someone can always come to help you, and there won't be as much of a risk of being talkative if someone [occasionally] helps you as there would be if you were to be together at all times.

In growing despondent from the toil, you find humility; and in finding humility, you receive remission of sins, for the Scripture says, "Behold my humility and my toil and forgive all

---

[15] Tr. note: "Give heed to yourself" (Gr: prosecho) is a refrain throughout the Book of Deuteronomy, introducing a reminder to be faithful to the covenant with God (Deut 6:12; 8:11; 11:16; 12:13; 12:19; 12:30; 15:9; 24:8). It became a central aspect of the monastic spirituality of St. Basil the Great.

my sins" (Ps 25:18). When you are humbled, you receive grace; and when you receive grace, the grace brings help to you; for St. Paul, having toiled more than all the other apostles, said, "Not I, but the grace of God that is with me" (1 Cor 15:10). If you believe without hesitation, you will be strengthened not only for the duty of gatekeeping, but also for other needs too. Attend on the work of God in hope, and in a manner you do not understand God will provide.

The brother then said, "Pray, father, that I may be given understanding and strength from God, since I am weak and unwise. The elder answered, "Brother, if you believe that God is able to raise children of Abraham from barren stones (Mt 3:9), that he opened the mouth of an ass [so that it could speak] (Num 22:21-39), believe too that he is able to fill your mouth with wisdom, to give you understanding and strength, and indeed that he will give you all these things. Brother, do you not understand these matters? The gate of the coenobium, it is the gate of God, and God knows that his servant the gatekeeper is in need of wisdom and understanding, of knowledge and strength, of help and discernment. "For your heavenly Father knows what you need before you ask him" (cf. Mt 6:8) as the Scripture says. If you endure and remain patient, your soul shall be blessed."

As far as I know, this brother was quite weak in body, hence he became exhausted doing this service by himself, even though it is not very difficult. At any rate, he now came to see all the [beneficial] things that would come to him from continuing this service because of what the God-bearing father had promised.

Principle 9
In what circumstances service should be preferred to prayer, and what kind of monk [should engage more in service.]

I. From Abba Mark

Our Lord, knowing that all things are fortified by prayer, says, "Do not be anxious about what you will eat, or what you will drink, or what you will wear, but seek first the kingdom of God, and all of these things will be added to you" (cf. Mt 6:25-34). And perhaps the Lord is also calling us to greater faith through these things. For who, in casting off anxiety for temporal matters and becoming free of needs, does not have faith in him and hope for eternal goods? The Lord makes this clear when he says, "He who is faithful in a little is also faithful in much" (cf. Lk 16:10). But in this he also shows his love for man, and since he knows that the daily provision for the flesh is necessary, he does not cut off everyday care[s], but in a manner truly befitting to God, he grants to us *this day*, while enjoining us not to be anxious about tomorrow. Since it is also impossible for us as human beings who are clothed in the flesh to completely discount bodily necessities.

Of course, it is possible to contract these into a small number of necessities through prayer and self-control, but to completely overlook them is impossible. Therefore, he who desires to "attain to mature manhood, to the measure of the stature of the fullness of Christ (Eph 4:13)" according to Scripture, should not prefer any tasks to prayer, neither should he engage in them unless absolutely necessary. But when he is presented with such a necessity or dispensation from God, neither should he shun or reject it under the pretext of prayer, but should learn both to distinguish between the proper times of prayer and service, and to serve the will of God unconditionally. And [it must be the case that] he who does not think in this manner neither believes in accordance with Scripture that, although each commandment is different from the others, they all complement/encompass each other, nor does he desire to *direct himself according to all the commandments* that arise by God's economy, as the Prophet says (cf. Psalm 118:128 LXX).

It is necessary, on the one hand, to accept required tasks that arise either unavoidably or by God's dispensation, and on the other hand, to give priority to prayer while refraining from unseasonable occupations, especially when these drag us down into luxury and avarice. The more a monk keeps these kinds of occupation in check, with the help of the Lord and by limiting the materials that feed into them, the more will he keep his mind from anxiety. And the more he keeps his anxiety in check, the more [freedom] he will have for pure prayer and faith in Christ. If someone is unable to do this out of lack of faith or owing to some other weakness, let him recognize the truth [of this] and exert himself in accordance with his strength, faulting himself for his own spiritual immaturity. For it is better at least to give an excuse based on one's own weakness, rather than a justification that is arrogant and deceptive.

In addition to what has been said, we are in need of much discernment from God, so as to know when we should prefer an errand to prayer, and which tasks warrant such attention, [particularly] because every monk is occupied with things that please himself, and thinks himself to be performing his duty, unaware that he should be choosing things that are pleasing to God rather than himself. Something that is yet more difficult to discern is the manner in which even the obligatory commandments are not to be done at all times, but some commandments should be preferred to others at certain times, since no task is done at all times, but each has its own appropriate season; nevertheless, it has been determined that the practice of prayer is to be unceasing (1 Th. 5:17). For this reason, we ought to prefer prayer to all occupations that are not [absolutely] necessary.

The Apostles all taught this distinction, for when the whole assembly [of Christians in Jerusalem] was trying to get them to be occupied with serving them, they said, "It is not right that we should give up preaching the word of God to serve tables. Therefore, brethren, pick out from among you seven men of good report, full of the Spirit and of wisdom, whom we will appoint to this duty. But we will continue to engage constantly in prayer and in the ministry of the word. And what they said pleased the whole gathering" (Act 6:2-5). What then do we learn from these things? Namely that, for those who are not yet able to engage constantly in prayer, it is good to be dedicated to service and to avoid falling away from both commandments; but for those who are able, it is better for them to devote themselves to the greater of these two [commandments, which is prayer].[16]

---

[16] Perhaps St. Mark implies here that the commandments of prayer and service respectively correspond to the "great commandments" to love God and to love your neighbor as yourself.

Principle 10
That a monk should arise for prayer eagerly and attend to it patiently.
Why the appointed times for prayer were originally established, and that monks should not disdain them.

I. From Gregory the Dialogist

At one of the monasteries founded by the servant of God Benedict, there was a brother who was troubled with the passion of slothfulness, and he couldn't endure standing alongside the other brothers during times of prayer, but while they would all be kneeling on the ground before God, he would be going outside and spending his time in chatter and idleness. His abbot, who had tried to counsel him but had accomplished nothing, decided to bring him directly to the man of God and there to accuse him of his vice. Thus, the holy father solemnly and formally reproved him for his slothfulness, and then sent him away after supporting him with counsel. After returning he followed the advice of the saint for just two days, but on the third day he reverted back to this demonic habit and began to wander off during the time of prayer. His abbot, seeing that he was once again conquered by the demon of acedia. He went to the saint again and told him about the brother, and the man of God said back, "I will come and correct him through my own example."

So he went to the monastery and stood with the brethren in the church, and when the singing of psalms was completed and the brothers had given themselves in prayer on bended knee, the saint looked up and there appeared to be a youth with the look of an Ethiopian, and he was tugging at the sleeve of the robe of that brother who was unable to persist in prayer, attempting to drag him out of the church. When the prayer was finished and the man of God departed from the place of prayer, he found the monk standing outside and for the blindness of his heart he struck him with a rod. From that time onward the brother was freed of his constant slothfulness, and for the rest [of his life] he earnestly stood alongside the brothers at the time of prayer until its completion, and the demon no longer dared to approach him, but stood afar off.

II. From the Life of St. John the Merciful

The blessed John, wishing to correct the laxity of those who were heedless during the divine services, did something worthy of remembrance. When he learned that many of the more negligent [churchgoers] exited the church after the reading of the holy gospels, he left the holy offering and he went out of the church, too, and sat with the whole crowd. When all the people were astonished at this, he said, "You should not marvel [at this], for wherever the sheep are, there too must be the shepherd in any case, for we are accustomed to doing these liturgies for you all, and for your benefit; but if you are busy mingling outside, this labor of ours is in vain. And so I persuaded myself to go outside with all of you, and to go back with you when you enter in again." This deed then provided correction to many people and liberated them from what had unfortunately become a custom.

III. From the Life of St. Pachomius

Once Pachomius the Great was teaching the monks under his guidance and, [wishing to] show the great benefit [of spiritual teaching], in the middle of his discourses he became ecstatic and stood like that for a long time. He then calmly said to the steward of the monastery, "Go to such-and-such a cell and learn who it is that is neglecting his own soul there, and be a witness to the harm he does to himself. For if it is the case that he hasn't come here to listen to the words of God so as to be strengthened against the demon that afflicts him (in the world/to go back to the world), [ask him] why he is not praying there, but rather sleeps? I do not know if he can [truly] be a monk." And [it happened] that after a little while that man did depart from the monks and left for the world, since he was unable to bear this lightest yoke of the Lord (cf. Mt 11:29-30).

IV. From the Gerontikon

1. An elder once said, "If you are doing a task in your cell and the hour of prayer comes, do not say to yourself, "I'll finish a few strands or a little basket first, and then I'll get up." But arise at that time and render your duty unto God, because [when] you gradually get accustomed to neglecting prayer and your service, your soul becomes barren of every work, both physical and spiritual; for your eagerness (will/should) make its appearance [first thing] in the morning.

2. They said about Abba Macarius that once, while he was on his way to the church to do a service, he beheld outside the cell of one of the brothers a throng of demons, some of which were in the form of women speaking improperly, some in the form of young men who also spoke nastily, while others were dancing and taking on various shapes. So then the elder in his clairvoyance understood the cause, and he sighed and said to himself, "This brother is always conducting his life heedlessly, and that's why the wicked spirits surround his cell like this."

After completing the service, then, he entered the brother's cell and said to him, "I am afflicted, brother, but nonetheless I have faith in you that if you pray for me God will alleviate my suffering. And he, repenting before the elder, said, "Father, I am not worthy of praying for you." But the elder insisted, beseeching the brother, saying, "I will not go away from here unless you give me your word that you will say one prayer for me every night." Then the brother was obedient to the elder's petition; the elder did this since he wanted to provide an incentive for him to pray at night.

It came to pass that the brother got up the following night and said a prayer for the elder; then he said to himself with contrition, "Wretched soul, you pray for this elder and are you not [even] praying for yourself?" Having done that he also said a long prayer for himself. He continued to do so every night, saying both of the prayers, and the following Sunday, when the elder was again on his way to church, he saw the demons standing outside the cell as they had been before, but they looked quite sad and gloomy. And he understood that the demons were saddened because of the brother's prayers. He was then filled with joy and went into the brother's cell and said, "Be charitable to me and add another prayer for me." And the brother was obedient and when he did the two prayers for the elder, he felt compunction again, and said to himself, "O miserable soul, add another prayer for yourself too."

Then he did so for that whole week, saying four prayers every night, and as the elder was passing by again on Sunday, he saw that the demons were even more distraught and completely silent, and he gave thanks to God, and as returned [from church] he went into the brother's cell again and asked him to add yet another prayer on his behalf. This too he graciously accepted, adding another prayer for himself and every night he said six prayers until the elder came again on Sunday and saw that the demons stood far off from his cell, and as they saw him going inside to see the brother, they raged at him since they were grieved by the salvation of the brother. But the elder glorified God, went inside and exhorted the brother not to be negligent, but to pray unceasingly (1 Th 5:17), and when the brother had become thus earnest in his prayers, by God's grace the demons departed from him altogether.

V. From St. Ephraim the Syrian

Brother, when a brother sounds the signal at night for you to rise up and worship God, eagerly arise so that even others who are more negligent may see your earnestness and arouse their souls to sobriety, like the [psalmist] who proclaims, "My eyes opened before dawn, that I might meditate on your utterances," and also, "At midnight I arose, to give thanks to you for the judgments of your righteousness" (Ps 118:148, 62 LXX). Have you not heard how the Prophet Samuel was called many times [in the night by God], and not once was he sluggish in arising, even though he was a child at the time? (I Sam 3). If it ever happens to you that you are possessed by a deep sleep, perhaps by demonic influence, and you miss part of the service, when you arise be wakeful, and do not be sluggish in going to the service by saying to yourself, "By now the service is almost at the dismissal, so why should I even go?"

Do not say such things, for such is the discourse of sluggards and idlers, but rather arise eagerly and hasten to the service, like one who is being pursued or like a gazelle fleeing from the hunters' nets. You should understand that just as those who go in the way of evil shall give an account of every idle word and speech in the day of judgment (Mt 12:36), so too everyone that runs toward the good shall receive a reward for each step [of the way] and for [every] good word. If then you make it in time for the later prayer, enter in and do not be ashamed; after all, you can confess what happened to the abbot, and then in your cell after the dismissal you may say those psalms which the influence of demons prevented you from praying (as long as you have the abbot's permission), and then the next night you will be more prepared for the work of the Lord. But if you neglect this [work] out of carelessness, and not due to some requirement or illness, you will do great harm to yourself.

Know this, too, beloved, that the more that one gives base comforts to his flesh, the more the passions multiply within him; and then the soul, when it is weighed down by the wicked habits of the body, becomes fruitless; hence the Savior says, "Be careful lest your hearts be weighed down with dissipation and drunkenness and cares of this life," (cf. Lk 21:34). For this reason too the Apostle says, "I discipline my body and bring it into subjection, lest after having preached to others I become disqualified myself " (1 Cor. 9:27). If, on the other hand, one subdues his body for the work of the Lord, it becomes all the healthier and the soul becomes radiant. For in the same way that an athlete needs to diligently train his body in order for it to meet the standards of the competition, likewise the contender in piety ought to train himself in every good work.

I also wish to say something to you about fatigue, and as I reckon, there are three causes of it. Firstly, when a monk begins to chant or pray, the Evil One immediately brings about fatigue in him, so that he will abandon the prayer and leave; but if he rouses himself and does not slack off, the demon can avail against him in nothing [acc. of resp.?]; and he will be much more bothered [by fatigue] if his stomach is heavy with food and drink. Secondly, fatigue from the same kind of negligence may come upon a monk in the middle of a service if he does not diligently push himself to concentrate until the completion of the rule and vainly thinks that it is no serious problem if he leaves behind those who are chanting to go to his bed or sit down to sleep outside. [Lastly], after the completion of the canon of the customary service, there occurs the fatigue which is natural, that is, when a brother is infirm, and we should pardon this, since it seems it is not unusual in the case of the infirm.

But you, brother, disdain not to "be sober in all things" (2 Tim 4:5), and while you stand during the service to worship our Lord and Savior Jesus Christ, either together with the brethren or by yourself, and the first kind of fatigue bothers you, as soon as you perceive it resist and bear persistently against it, and even if overcomes you at first, once or twice, do not depart from your place, and you will find great profit. For the passion of insatiable sleep is like gluttony: since, when someone is addicted to eating a lot, his bodily nature will demand much; but if someone is accustomed to self-control, neither does his bodily nature require much food; it is the same in the case of sleep. How are you so bold as to leave the service and go out before the dismissal without any serious need? If then, brother, you were invited to the supper of a wealthy man, would you dare get up from the midst of those who are dining together and go home? Would you not remain seated until everyone gets up together?

Therefore, beloved, let us fear the Master of both Heaven and Earth; let us be earnest to be well-pleasing to him, since it is written: "Cursed is everyone who does the work of the Lord negligently" (cf. Jer 48:10 [31:10 LXX]). Consider the fishermen, how they spend every night in vigil, persisting in their work; and if any of them gets weighed down with sleep and dozes off out of carelessness, once he wakes up from his sleep he understands that he didn't catch anything, while the others stayed awake had gotten resources, and then he begins to feel regret in himself and says, "Woe to me, careless and indolent as I am, for in taking ease I fell asleep, and look I return now empty-handed; as [the Scripture] says "they have slept their sleep and have found nothing [in their hands]" (Ps 75:5 LXX).

Also bring to mind the potters and those skilled in the art of brass making, and there too you will find an immeasurable amount of labor, as well as great and intense vigilance. Moreover, they endure this kind of labor and toil for the works of this age, while we endure nothing toilsome or unpleasant; but we, who stand in a pure and sanctified place before the Lord our God in great peace and solemnity, spiritual rejoicing and good hope, why do we idle and slack off? Why do we not rather raise ourselves up for the sweetest worship of our Lord and Savior? For David says, "How sweet to my throat are your utterances, sweeter than honey to my mouth!" and again, "My lips shall rejoice when I chant to you, and my soul, which you have redeemed" (Ps 70:23 LXX).

After all, how much is our time on this earth, that we so neglect our salvation? Behold, the same prophet cries aloud, "Man has become like vanity, as a shadow do his days pass by" (Ps 143:4 LXX). So do not contend with me, beloved servant of Christ, who am negligent and impatient, knowing well that he who keeps sobriety will obtain benefit, and he who is negligent will suffer harm; for each of us will give an account of himself to God. Moreover, do not consider sleep and the body's relaxation as gain, but instead as the greatest loss. For the kingdom of God is [what is to be gained].

Let us push ourselves then, beloved ones, in order to attain the Kingdom and [Christ's] blessedness, as he said, "Blessed are those servants whose Lord finds them watching when he comes" (Lk 12:37). And [this is not only meant for] ourselves, but [so that] through love [we may] exhort and encourage one another in the fear of the Lord, and that we may stir up each other's eagerness to glorify our God and Savior Jesus Christ; so that we may receive, not only for ourselves but also for our neighbor's benefit, those abundant rewards from hm who said, "Inasmuch as you have done so to one of the least of these my brethren, you have done it to me" (Mt 25:40).

VI. From Abba Isaiah

When you arise in your cell to do your rule of prayer, see that you do not disdain it in negligence, lest instead of honoring God you end up angering him; rather stand in the fear of God. Do not lean against the wall and do not make your feet idle by shifting your weight onto the one and easing the other like a buffoon. And keep your heart from getting caught up in your [mind's] deliberations, so that God may accept your sacrifice.

VII. From the Order of Peter and Paul

Conduct prayers at dawn, the third hour, the sixth hour, the ninth hour, in the evening, and at the rooster's crow. At dawn, because [at that time] the Lord shines light upon us, and after producing the night he brings about the day. And at the third hour, since because at that time Christ received the judgment from Pilate; and at the sixth hour, because at that time he was crucified; at the ninth hour, because at that time all things trembled at the crucifixion of their Master, were terrified by the audacity of the impious Jews, unable to bear the humiliation of their Lord. And at evening because at that time he provides us the night for rest from our everyday labors; and finally, at the cry of the rooster, because at that hour is announced the good news of the new day's coming, that we may accomplish the works of light.

Principle 11
Concerning chant and prayer, how to keep good order in regard to them.

I. From the Gerontikon

I. Abba Pambo sent his disciple to sell his crafts. This he did for sixteen days, as he used to tell me, and during the nights he slept in the church narthex at the Church of the Holy Apostle Mark, and saw the church services, and by the time he returned to the Elder he had even learned troparia hymns. Thus the elder said to him, "I see that you are not at peace, child. Has some temptation occurred to you in the city?" The brother replied, "Abba, we generally waste our days away here in the desert, and we don't even chant canons or troparia; I saw how the church choirs chant when I went to the city, and I became very sorrowful because we don't chant canons and troparia like they do.

The elder said to him, "Woe to us, child! For the days have come when monks abandon the solid food which was spoken of through the Holy Spirit (cf. Heb 5:14), and now they are eager for songs and tunes. What compunction and what tears are born from troparia, from raising your voice like cattle, whether you are standing in a church or in a cell? For if we stand before God, we ought to stand in great compunction, and not in our own exaltation. For monks did not come out into the desert here to exalt themselves while standing in the presence of God by singing songs, modifying tones, shaking their hands and shifting their feet; we should be offering our prayers to God in fear and trembling before God, in tears and sighs, with a voice that is reverent, moderate and humble.

For behold I tell you, my child, the days are coming when Christians will corrupt the books of the Sacred Gospels, of the Holy Apostles, and of the Divine Prophets, glossing over the Holy Scriptures, and [they will] write troparia hymns and Greek words/discourses, and shall pour [their] intellect into these, but they will be far from the others [the Scriptures]. For this reason our Fathers have said that while being in the desert they would not write the lives and sayings of the Fathers on parchment, but on paper, because the next generation is going to varnish lives of the Fathers and write according to their own will, and there will be a dire need.

And the brother said to him, "What then? Will the customs and traditions of Christians be altered? And for this to happen will there cease to be priests in the church?" And the elder said, "In such times the love of many will grow cold (Mt 24:12), and there will be no little affliction, invasions of nations and migrations of peoples, instability among kings, profligacy among priests, and negligence among monastics. There shall be church leaders who will neglect their own salvation, and that of their flock, eager to hasten off to dinners, quarrelsome, lazy in prayer and disposed to evil gossip. [They will be] quick to condemn the lives and sayings of the elders, and will neither imitate them nor listen to them, but instead will slander and say, 'If we had been living in their days, we would have struggled like them, too.'

"Moreover, the bishops in those days will fear those in power, giving judgments on bribes, refusing to defend the poor in trials, afflicting widows and grieving orphans, and then shall there enter in among the people disbelief, hatred, enmity, jealousy, strife, thefts and drunken revels."

Then the brother said, "What then must one do in those times and seasons?" And the elder said, "My child, in days such as those, let him who wishes to be saved look to the salvation of his own soul, and he shall be called great in the Kingdom of Heaven.

II. From the Life of St. Luke the New

St. Luke once went to visit one of the well-known monks, who was himself a devout man acting as shepherd of God-loving men. He stayed with him until he was possessed with a longing on the third day to return to his hut in the desert; however, when he asked to depart the abbot didn't give him permission; for he in turn had a great longing to keep him there, and he couldn't tolerate being parted from him, it being the case that the affection of those who love according to God are even more intense than that of relatives in the world. When he did not [accept this and] simply take leave, but rather expressly insisted on returning, the abbot used an approaching feast day as a reason to keep him there, and being stirred by his affection, he spoke to him in a somewhat harsher tone, "For how long will you remain in those wild environs, and prefer the desert to the church gathering? Now this great feast is already at the doors, and if you miss the opportunity to liturgize, will it not be a grave loss for you?"

To all of this the God-bearing father replied with that fair and blessed simplicity which was characteristic of him, "Good teacher, blessed shepherd, you say well. But these rules and readings, and indeed all the church services, if it is the case that they must warrant our attention, what is it that they all lead to? It would seem that their goal, as you yourself teach, is to lead us to the fear of God, and to raise up to God those who keep to them attentively. As for the one who has already diligently acquired the fear of God in his heart, what need has he of the things you speak of?" Upon hearing this, the abbot greatly admired St. Luke for his good defense, and no longer desired to keep him, he immediately let him return to his dwelling.

III. From St. Diadochos

In the abundance of its natural fruits, the soul chants with a stronger voice, and she desires to pray aloud more. But when she is moved by the Holy Spirit, she chants and prays with abundant ease and sweetness, with the whole heart. In the former case, there follows a visible joy, while in the latter case there are spiritual tears, and after this there comes an inner jubilation that gives rise to a love of inner tranquility. For warm is the recollection of that harmony of chanting that remains in the soul, and it brings thoughts to the heart that give rise to tears and tranquility; from these things, one can see the seeds of prayer being sown with tears in the soil of his heart, with joy on account of the hope of the harvest.

Nevertheless, when we are weighed down with intense despondency, it is a little more necessary to chant in a louder voice and to make the cords of the soul resound with the joy of hope, until that burdensome cloud is dissipated by the winds of melody.

IV. From Abba Cassian

All the eastern cenobitic communities, especially the Egyptian ones, have a rule for prayers and chants of this kind: Whenever the brethren are gathered together in one place for the liturgy, as soon as the chanting is finished, they do not proceed immediately to kneeling, but before bending their knees, they first pray for a short time standing with their hands outstretched. Then after this they prostrate on the ground to pray on their knees for a while, but no one goes to kneel or rises up until the one who is leading them in prayer has first done so.

When the brothers come together for these services I have described, there is produced a silence among them so great that one might think there that there is no man present, despite there being so numerous a multitude of brethren. And it is extraordinary that during this time of prayer, [you can't hear] any swallowing or coughing, idling or yawning from fatigue, or any sound of sighing. And they say that he who does his prayers languorously and obnoxiously sins doubly, first, because he is praying slothfully, and second, because with his uncontrolled voice he not only annoys (the hearing) of the others, but distracts their attention/intellect too, when they are [at the same time] being assaulted by the wicked demons, who in seeing us standing at prayer, burden our soul with inappropriate thoughts and despondency. For this same reason, the monks make sure to chant psalms without noise and commotion, not in the exuberance of many verses, but in the rejoicing of the intellect's activity/focus, and so they follow precisely that word which is spoken, "I will chant with the spirit, I will chant with my mind also" (1 Cor 14:15). For they regard it as more beneficial to chant ten verses with understanding, rather than the whole psalm with confusion in their mind (cf. 1 Cor 14:19).

And when the canon and psalms are completed as we have said above, none of the brothers dare even to stand for a little or to speak with another, but they go to their own cells and persist in the work which each does with his own hands, fulfilling the apostolic injunction.[17] And during the time of the liturgy, as well as the third, sixth, and ninth hours, if someone does not arrive before the first psalm is finished, he does not dare enter the building or go to the choir. Rather, he stands at the doors and waits till the dismissal of the brothers, and when they all leave, he prostrates himself on the ground and seeks forgiveness for his slothfulness. As for the night services, they are allowed to be late only until the second psalm.

V. From the Gerontikon

1. Abba Macarius the Great used to say to the brothers after church finished, "Flee, brethren!" [Thus once] one of the elders asked him, "Father, where do we have to flee to, being in this desert?" Then placing his finger on his mouth, he said, "Flee from *this*." He then went to his cell, closed the door, and remained there.

2. They used to say about Abba Sisoes from Thebes that after church ended, he would immediately rush off to his cell, walking hastily and looking like someone who was running away, and thus some of those that saw him acting like this would say, "He has a demon." But he was doing the work of God and paid no attention to those who told tales against him.

3. A brother once asked for advice from Abba Silouan, saying, "What shall I do? How shall I acquire compunction? For I am very troubled by despondency,

---

[17] "We beseech you, brethren, that ye increase more and more; and to aspire to live quietly, and to mind your own affairs, and to work with your hands, as we instructed you" (1 Th 4:10-11.

sleep and yawning, and when I arise from sleep, I struggle a great deal in psalmody and can't shake off my drowsiness, neither can I say any psalm without singing it out loud. Then the elder answered him, "Child, first of all, for you to sing the psalms aloud is pride, since that would mean that you can chant while your brother cannot. Secondly, it hardens your heart and doesn't allow room for (compunction. Therefore, if you desire compunction, abandon the singing, and while you stand to do your prayers, let your nous concentrate on the power of the verse, and consider how you are standing before the presence of God, "who examines the hearts and the reins" (Ps 7:10). And when you arise from sleep, before doing anything else, let your mouth glorify God, either by stating the faith or saying the Our Father, and then calmly begin your rule, sighing and remembering your sins and the punishment you deserve to be tormented with.

The brother then said, "Abba, ever since I became a monk, I have been chanting the services of the canon and hours in the eight tones." And the elder replied, "And it is for this reason that compunction and grief flee from you. Bring to mind how those great Fathers, who being uneducated did not learn tones and troparia, but perhaps a few psalms, and how they shined as lights in the world. For example, there was Abba Paul the Simple, and Abba Pambo, and Abba Apollo, and the rest of the God-bearing Fathers, who raised the dead and performed great miracles and received authority against demons, not through songs and troparia and tones, but through prayer with a broken heart and by fasting; by these the fear of God comes to dwell in the heart unceasingly, and that grief is fortified which cleanses man from every sin and renders his intellect whiter than snow (cf. Ps 50.9 LXX).

"Singing has brought many down to the lowest parts of the earth, not only laypeople, but even priests, and it emasculated them and launched them into fornication and other shameful passions. So then, singing is for people in the world, and the people gather in churches to hear it. But consider, my child, how many ranks of angels are in heaven, and it is not written concerning any of them that they sing in the eight tones, but one order chants "Alleluia" unceasingly, while another sings "Holy, Holy, Holy Sabaoth", and yet another, "Blessed be the glory of the Lord from his place and his house" (cf. Ezek. 3:12). Thus, my child, imitate the Fathers if you desire to acquire contrition in your prayers, and keep your mind from wandering, as much as you can. Love the humility of Christ and wherever you happen to go, do not present yourself as an intelligent teacher, but as an unlearned disciple, and God will provide you with compunction."

4. An elder once said, "Those who pray to God should do their prayer in peace, in great silence and composure[18], and they certainly shouldn't disturb themselves or their neighbors with inappropriate and confused cries and yells, but should focus on the Lord with pain of heart and sober thoughts. In the same way that, among those who have bodily ailments, there are some who bear the pain of the cautery or the surgery courageously and patiently, without crying out or shaking. They retain control of themselves despite the pains of medicine, enduring in silence. Then there are others who, when they suffer the same things, react with inappropriate cries and tremors, although the pain is the same for both those who cry out and those who do not, and so it is with prayers and compunction. There are some who pray in stillness[19] and preserve the tension of the heart in greater tranquility, and others who have no self-possession, but do their prayers in an agitated and noisy manner, so as even to scandalize those who hear them. But a servant of God should not be found in such discomposure, but rather in all

---

[18] καταστάσει
[19] ησυχία

humble mindedness and silence, just as God says in the Prophet Isaiah, "Whom shall I look upon, but on him who is meek and silent and trembles at my words?" (Is 66:2). For those who conduct themselves in this manner edify all those who see them.

VI. From St. Ephraim

It is good and salvific to be at the service before everyone else; but to leave the service before the dismissal without good reason is harmful and destructive. Thus, attend to and hear the Divine Scriptures so as to be benefited. For, in the same way that a cool drink is pleasant to a man traveling in the heat, so the Divine Words are refreshing to the soul. If you desire to hear them, attend to them, and if you listen to them you shall be wise. But if you can hardly have the patience to hear the word, how much harder will the practice be. Therefore, come to know yourself through this, to know that you are remiss, in the way that I do myself.

And when you are all going into the house of the Lord, let all exaltation stand afar off from your minds, and let your inner person rest in contemplation and prayer, so that no foreign thoughts disturb your intellect.

Let us realize who it is we stand before in prayer, and let all our soul and heart incline towards him, imagining nothing else. Understand what we speak of from an example, too: when a man goes to the bazaar with a pouch of money intent on buying oxen, will he go examine the pigs? And if he desires to purchase donkeys, will he look for dogs? Isn't all his thinking directed to the goods he desires, and won't he go survey them alone, lest he be defrauded and spend his money for no purpose. In the same way, whenever we go into the sacred house to stand before God, we too should raise our minds to God, and let us think on and contemplate the things that pertain to him, so that in this manner we may purchase our salvation and enjoy the heavenly goods. Furthermore, we should not be sidetracked by any conversation with the person next to us, lest we end up angering the Maker of heaven and earth instead of obtaining his mercy.

For, just as someone who is standing and speaking in the king's presence would insult the king himself and incur his terrible wrath if he were to spurn the king's marvelous and glorious speech when his fellow servant calls on him and turn to converse with him instead, so it is much the same in the case of the person who talks during the time of chanting and prayer. In the same way that the angels stand and conduct their hymns to the Creator with much trembling, so we too should stand and chant before [God]. If perhaps the brother standing near you, being infirm in body, coughs or spits a lot, don't be irritated by him, but remember that many have dedicated themselves to serve the sick and lepers, dismembered) to be greatly benefited by this, learning love and sympathy by experience. And you too are clad, as it were, in the same kind of body; you [too] are susceptible to these sorts of illnesses, even if at present you are healthy in body by [the grace] of God's love toward man. Therefore do not elevate yourself above the infirm, but fear lest you suffer the same things or worse, and secure yourself through sympathy toward [your] brother.

Principle 12
That it is necessary to reprove those who chatter or socialize during the divine services, and if they do not amend their behavior, they should be strictly removed from the church.

I. From the Life of St. John the Merciful

The great John made sure to correct those who would mindlessly socialize in Church as much as he could; if he saw someone who after the first and second had still not improved, he would immediately cast him out of the church, echoing the voice of the Lord with his words, "The house of God should be a house of prayer" (Mt 21:13, Mk 11:17, Lk 19:46). But again, he [gladly] accepted those who were more attentive concerning the divine services and praised them for their love of God, and even honored them with ranks for their progress.

II. From the Gerontikon

1. An elder once said, "If anybody happens to be in church, whether he is with many others or few, and he keeps his mouth from crying aloud to God, he is doing the work of demons; for the demons cannot stand to hear Christ being praised, and they prevent people from chanting.

2. Abba Evagrius said, "It is a great thing to pray without distraction; but it is even greater to chant without distraction."

III. From St. Ephraim

Brother, when you stand in the house of the Lord for spiritual worship, be earnest in chanting; for if you keep silent, I too will (might) become silent, and then the other person beside you, and then by necessity the chanting will cease. But do not let it come to [this point]. As it is with those who applaud a prince or king, when they are standing in the theater and see someone in their midst who is just standing without crying aloud with a raised voice, they push him and drive him away, judging him to be unworthy of this kind of event/ standing with them; and how much more then should we enthusiastically stand before the Lord of Heaven and Earth, and earnestly sing our chants to him? But be careful that you do not upset a group of disciplined men while they are standing and praising the Lord, lest God-sent wrath and injury fall upon you. For to sin against God is dangerous and inexcusable, and as it is written, "the spirits of prophets are subject to prophets; for God is not a God of confusion but of peace." (1 Cor 14:31-33)

IV. Antiochus Pandectus[20]

Chanting is the work of the incorporeal hosts, who serve God unceasingly in his presence, as it is said, "Praise the Lord from the heavens, all ye his angels; praise him, all ye his hosts" (Ps 148:2 LXX). This is befitting to all men and women, too, for the Scripture says, "Let every breath praise the Lord", and especially to monastics who assume the angelic life, for it says, "Ye that fear the Lord, praise him; all ye seed of Jacob, glorify him" (Ps 21:24 LXX).

So then, chanting is a continual sacrifice and a sacrifice of praise, as it is written: "a sacrifice of praise will glorify me" (Ps 49:23). Therefore, we monks are obliged to continually and unceasingly render unto God the appointed doxologies, hearing David who instruct us,

---

[20] Πανδέκτης των Θεοπνευστών Αγίων Γραφών : εν ω κεφαλαία ή λόγοι ΡΛ (130) και περί προσευχής και εξομολογήσεως -- BR65.A48 1991

saying, "Sing to our God, sing ye; sing to our king, sing ye. Sing with understanding to the Lord ye his servant.

But why is it necessary to quote all of David's testimonies concerning chanting or the joy and gladness that arises in the heart of the one who chants with compunction and sobriety? For those who are experienced understand exactly [what is meant]. Let us then stand well in psalmody and prayer, beloved ones, turning away from the influence of thoughts and cares. For the demons, whenever they see someone chanting or praying earnestly, are in the habit of insinuating the thought of things seemingly necessary, stirring the mind to engage with them so that through being preoccupied it will lose the sweetness of chanting. Hence Christ "perfects praise through the mouth of babes" (Ps 8:3 LXX), that is, those who are babes in their innocence, so that through psalmody he might abolish the enemy who tyrannizes us, the vindictive devil, who is the adversary of virtues and the avenger of wickedness.

And we, when we praise the Lord in simplicity, are crushing and abolishing his devices. Therefore let the chant be constant, for when God is but named, it causes the demons to flee. And it is necessary for you to remember this also, that our chanting is called a rule, as you yourselves know. So just as a farmer suffers many terrible things when he fails to render his *rule*, or measure, good and complete, and he is put in prison, racked and skinned until he renders all his dues, likewise when the monk neglects to keep his rule, he is immediately forsaken by grace, given over to his enemies, and trampled under their feet.

V. From Abba Isaiah

Brethren, do not say anything at trapeza or at a service when is no great need, and do not correct anyone while he is chanting, in case he turns and asks you what [is wrong]. For if anyone makes an error in some word and goes on reading, after all it is merely a word. You should not be hasty to point it out to him and disturb him; but if he says, "Do me a favor and tell me," then you may tell him.

VI. From St. Ephraim

Brother, if you do not wish to build up/edify [others?], do not break down what has already been built up. If you do not wish to plant, do not uproot what has been planted; which is to say, if while standing at a service you do not wish to send up hymns to the Lord, [at least] do not prevent those who are chanting. A rich man speaks, and everybody grows silent, and they exalt his speech to the clouds; then God speaks to us through the Divine Scriptures and we do not wish to be silent and listen? But one person chats, while another dozes off, and another is wandering about in his thoughts. However, what does the Scripture say? "He that turns away his ear from hearing the law of the most high, both he and his prayer shall be abominable before God" (cf. Pr 28:9 LXX).

Careless is the monk that is eager to hear the Amen while praying. But the one who prays soberly does so without boredom or agitation. And there was once something said by a Prophet that concerns us, "You are near to their lips, but far from their reins" (cf. Jer 12:2). O monk, the brethren stand at liturgy blessing God, and are you are occupied [with things] outside? Do you not realize that you are bringing harm to yourself? Say to your thought, "If this had to do with an offer of gold or some other material good, wouldn't we hasten to be there before everyone else? And if fleshly goods arouse so much interest, how much more should spiritual goods?" Be fervent in spirit as the saints were, that you might dwell together with them in the courts of the Kingdom of Heaven.

Printed in Great Britain
by Amazon